Seeking the One Whom We Love

How RSCJs Pray

Seeking the One Whom We Love

How RSCJs Pray

Edited by Kathleen Hughes, RSCJ and Therese Fink Meyerhoff

Seeking the One Whom We Love
How RSCJs Pray

Edited by Kathleen Hughes, RSCJ and Therese Fink Meyerhoff

Book design by Peggy Nehmen, n-kcreative.com

Printed in the United States of America
ISBN-13: 978-0-9971329-0-8

Published by:

Society of the Sacred Heart™
United States – Canada

4120 Forest Park Avenue
St. Louis Missouri 63108-2809
314-652-1500
www.rscj.org

These essays are dedicated to Saint Madeleine Sophie Barat and Saint Rose Philippine Duchesne, women whose ceaseless search for the One whom they loved has drawn countless Religious of the Sacred Heart to emulate them in their longing for God and their life of prayer.

Contents

*Throughout the collection, an asterisk has been used when a word or phrase may not be immediately clear, inviting the reader to consult the glossary.

Acknowledgments

We wish to acknowledge with gratitude all of the people who made this book possible:

The Religious of the Sacred Heart who responded to our invitation to write about their experience of prayer;

Frances Gimber, RSCJ, and the members of the Publications Committee of the United States – Canada Province of the Society of the Sacred Heart for their encouragement and editorial support;

Dolores Schuh, HM, meticulous proofreader;

Peggy Nehmen, of Nehmen-Kodner, for book design, thoughtful interpretation of our subject matter and self-publishing guidance;

Regina Shin, RSCJ, artist, for use of her watercolor, *Reflections*, on the cover;

Marie Howe, graduate of the Academy of the Sacred Heart, Rochester, for permission to include her poem "Annunciation" from her collection, *The Kingdom of Ordinary Time*, published by W. W. Norton and Company;

And our dear friend, Patricia Rosemary Peeler, graduate of the Academy of the Sacred Heart, Grosse Pointe and Manhattanville College, who taught at Manhattanville College, the Convent of the Sacred Heart, Greenwich, Connecticut, and the Convent of the Sacred Heart, 91st Street, New York City. Educator, friend, musician, volunteer and benefactor, Rosemary died from cancer April 12, 2013. Her generous bequest made the publication of *Seeking the One Whom We Love* possible.

Introduction

What difference does it make how you pray,
provided that your heart is seeking the One whom you love?

—*Saint Madeleine Sophie Barat*

Prayer is a profound mystery.

It is utterly mysterious that we can be in relationship with God, that we can be drawn into the very life of God. It is beyond imagining that God has planted this desire for intimacy in our hearts. It is a mystery that this yearning for union is a mutual love and longing, God's and ours, a mutual thirst and desire, every bit as much on God's part as on ours. And because prayer is essentially about relationship, there are as many ways of praying as there are human hearts turned to the divine.

Still, certain patterns emerge. Certain "schools of prayer" have developed over the centuries. Certain spiritual guides have provided ways of prayer consistent with their particular understanding of God and of the holy life.

The founder of the Society of the Sacred Heart of Jesus, Saint Madeleine Sophie Barat, never wrote a treatise on prayer. Nevertheless, her "school of prayer" can be gleaned from notes of the numerous spiritual talks she gave, often in tandem with the feasts and seasons of the church year, and from more than fourteen thousand letters she wrote to Religious of the Sacred Heart and to spiritual guides, authorities of church and state, family and friends of the Society of the Sacred Heart.

Her school of prayer is captured in one deceptively simple phrase – prayer and the interior life – a phrase enshrined in the original Constitutions and Rules of the Society of the Sacred Heart of Jesus, which she prepared with Joseph Varin, SJ, in 1815:

> *The spirit of the Society*
> *is essentially based upon prayer and the interior life*
> *since we cannot glorify the adorable*
> *Heart of Jesus worthily*
> *except inasmuch as we apply ourselves*
> *to study His interior dispositions*
> *in order to unite and conform ourselves to them.*

—(Abridged Plan, §5)

Sophie, as she was known to family and friends, had a lifelong attraction to contemplation, which led her, so often, to speak of prayer and the interior life in the same breath, referring to the specific practice of prayer on the one hand and to prayer as a habit of heart and a way of life on the other. Always, for Sophie, both prayer and the interior life were means to an end. The end of prayer was to put on the mind and heart of Christ; the end was a gradual and imperceptible but sure transformation in love. In Sophie's school of prayer, being changed into the Beloved happens over time, with mindfulness and silence and the cultivation of an inner world – prayer and the interior life joined to sustain such transformation.

Sophie had a fundamental conviction: prayer, strictly speaking, flourishes in a person who, at the deepest level of her being, lives in union with God and longs for more complete identification. Interior spirit is a habitual mindfulness, a deep life of presence, and everything that nurtures one's environment so that a life of union with God is possible. Praying, at its heart, is loving, and the one loved is never far from one's consciousness, even in the midst of a very busy life.

For Sophie, all forms of prayer and every manner of discipline surrounding prayer were simply ways of deepening one's personal relationship with God, of entering into that experience of mutual love and longing that prompted Christ by the side of the well to name his thirst, and a woman to welcome the waters Christ offered.

Prayer is relationship, as simple as that. At one time Sophie wrote to a friend: "What difference does it make how you pray, provided that your heart is seeking the One whom you love?" Though she spoke repeatedly of various forms of prayer and ways to prepare, of attentiveness and silence and self-forgetfulness, of methods and practices of recollection, all of it was only a means. Sophie was very free, and she freed others, to find the ways they were drawn to God by their particular natures and temperaments.

There were certain times and forms of prayer laid out in the Constitutions for those under Sophie's care, but she recognized that each one has a unique relationship with God. Her letters breathe a spirit of astonishing freedom as she encouraged those of varying backgrounds, ages and personalities to find their path to communion with God.

Sophie knew there is no one perfect way to pray but only a longing deep in each heart for the divine, a desire nourished by the power of the Holy Spirit who groans within each one with cries too deep for words. At the same time, she knew that prayer is a craft requiring discipline and practice, especially for beginners. In her conferences and letters, while Sophie clearly shows the greatest freedom in allowing each one to adopt a manner of prayer suited to her temperament and leanings, she was also aware that much self-delusion is possible in the spiritual life and especially in the practice of prayer. One can think one is praying and actually be engaged in other activities altogether, in having a fascinating conversation with oneself, for example, or carefully planning the day ahead.

Because there are endless possibilities of self-delusion in prayer, Sophie offered a few disciplines and safeguards. In her letters to superiors and to directors of formation she often urged them to help those they guided to learn to talk about their prayer, a topic about which there is sometimes a remarkable reticence. On the one hand, some seem incapable of finding words to describe something ineffable and precious; on the other hand, some seem truly apprehensive, perhaps believing "… everyone else really knows how to pray while I just muddle along." Finding a wise mentor or exchanging experiences of prayer with trusted spiritual directors or friends was for Sophie a wonderful learning experience, a testing of the Spirit, a safeguard against various illusions.

The gift of Sophie's school of prayer is twofold. There is, first, her conviction that prayer is as necessary and as natural to the human heart as breathing in and breathing out; it is a deep desire for union with God, a mutual exchange of love and longing, a relationship unique to each one of us with God. Many spiritual writers say much the same thing. But it is her second gift, her emphasis on interior life, that makes her school of prayer distinctive – her insistence on prayer as a habit of heart, a way of living, a way of relating to others, of using time, of filling the imagination. Interior life is living always with a deep consciousness, even in the midst of great activity, that God is more present to us than we are to ourselves, always drawing us God-ward.

Prayer and the interior life are the two aspects of union with God, two facets of the spiritual life that Sophie hoped would transform the lives of all her followers, all of us who are drawn to her vision and her mission, so that each one might one day say: "I live now, not I, but Christ lives in me."

Sophie's school of prayer is remarkably well illustrated in the essays that follow. Fifty-five Religious of the Sacred Heart of the United States – Canada Province responded to an invitation to write about their prayer. These are not reflections about what we have read about prayer or what we think about prayer. They are, rather, glimpses of the way each one has nurtured and sustained her relationship with God.

The essays vary in length and style. Some include a poem or prayer, a pencil sketch, a few charts, a water color, a series of photographs. Interspersed among the essays are also precious insights about prayer from some of our founding mothers: Sophie herself, Saint Rose Philippine Duchesne, and Mother Janet Erskine Stuart. There are also brief citations about prayer from the *Constitutions of the Society of the Sacred Heart*, those written in 1815, and those of 1982, written after the Second Vatican Council (1962-1965), which asked religious women and men to rearticulate their charism for today. An appendix contains the whole chapter on prayer from the 1982 Constitutions. Throughout the collection, an asterisk has been used when a word or phrase may not be immediately clear, inviting the reader to consult a glossary of terms in an appendix.

While the essays differ in almost every way, there are a few striking commonalities. For one thing, they illustrate that deep longing for God and a contemplative way of life that was also Sophie's passion. They also illustrate a commitment to a life of prayer, in times of struggle every bit as much as times of consolation and delight. Above all, the bedrock of these essays is what binds Religious of the Sacred Heart together: a common search for the One whom we love, a struggle with the tension of being wholly contemplative and wholly apostolic, and a longing to make God's love visible in the heart of the world.

Kathleen Hughes, RSCJ

Therese Fink Meyerhoff

Editors

Living from the Inside Out

Bridget Bearss, RSCJ

Without the sun, the colors of the stained glass windows are not revealed. The shadow is darkest where the sun shines directly. One thing depends on the other. I have learned to live the contemplative life from the activity of my life, and activity becomes contemplation. For me, activity came first.

My first vocation was the call of an educator. Well, actually, my very first vocation was the call of the land.

We are farm people ... where early lessons are about planting and harvesting and the clear recognition that the outcome does not necessarily match the effort. Famine and feast are equally possible, and there are no guarantees. Perhaps that's a good lesson for the life lived in the land of love that I call Detroit. Here we have learned lessons about vulnerability, knowing that we "reap what we sow," and making every decision the one that makes the gospel visible.

It is here, in this house built on confidence, that I have learned to breathe the lessons of contemplation and action. I entered the Society of the Sacred Heart because I had learned to love in the fields of Nebraska, and that love was translated into a desire to change the world. That desire found form in the work of education. It never occurred to me that I needed to enter the Society of the Sacred Heart to be part of the mission. Like the land of my heritage and my love of the work of education, my family was part of the Society and the Society was part of my family. My heart was formed by the Religious of the Sacred Heart in the life we shared with my two beloved aunts, Eileen and Rosemary Bearss, both RSCJs. It was in my relationship to them that the early seeds of contemplation were planted by attraction, not promotion, to a life that was intentional, authentic and fundamentally rooted in love. But it never occurred to me that I needed to enter the Society to belong.

I entered the Society as a passionate teacher – a faculty member at Duchesne Academy in Houston. I wanted to change the world through the liberation of thought that comes through the work of education. I was swept away with Sophie Barat's vision that resonated with mine: building bridges of relationship between people of difference. I had long known the Jesus of activism and social change, and I had visions of the difference it would make to educate in such a way that God's dream for us became our dream for the world.

My early life in the post-Vatican II and post-Vietnam world taught me much more about political activity, equality and ways to make lasting change than it did about doctrine. To envision a new way of collaboration that creates a world worthy of our children left me with a fire in my heart and a readiness to build a new world. Action was my invitation. Contemplation was the gift that discovered me.

I entered the Society without letters of theological accomplishment, but I was teachable, and my desire was met with love. I was given a new way of living – from the inside out – that transformed the fire I knew for the work of education into the source of that flame. I learned to sit in the stillness and to learn to live what Rosemary taught me about the connection between action and contemplation. She used to tell me to follow my heart and remember that "it is like a single breath . . . action and contemplation . . . one leads to the other in a single movement, never separate."

Here in Detroit, where we have watched worlds tumble down and where there is no going back to what was, I have learned the story of the phoenix that rises and the real meaning of resurrection. My time of daily sitting in the stillness of not knowing is my way. It is not remarkable or distinctive or full of spectacular revelations. It is the simple action of sitting still with God and letting God be God. I have learned to live my life of trust in God's grace that shows up at exactly the moment that I need it, not ten seconds before.

Here, I have been taught to love in ways that you don't find in administration manuals, and I have discovered our Constitutions. Sitting in bankruptcy court with one who once was a major donor, receiving a voluntary pay cut from a faculty member, looking forward to a new future that we create together, watching the children who will change the world because they know that absolutely everything is a gift . . . here I often lose track of which is contemplation and which is action. Sometimes I wonder which is the prayer . . . my long hours of doing what I love more than I could have imagined or the hour a day I spend sitting in silence and being in the presence of my God of love. I can't figure out which is which: is it action that follows contemplation or contemplation that follows action?

And then I remember the Jesus that I first fell in love with when I was sixteen and needed someone to show me the pathway through a perilous time of terror as the whole world seemed to forget the values of integrity, trust and sanity. And I recall the

God of the wheat field when my dad first explained to me how God and the wheat of our harvest were the same:

> When we grow wheat, something has to die so that
> something else can live. If we don't cut the wheat,
> it can't make the bread of life. Don't worry. We
> are all like that. We are planted and harvested and
> then we become something else. It's how God is.

There are lots of things I don't know. But I know a lot about the difference that education makes in the life of a child and a family and a world. And I know what it means to love from the inside out in a city that some people have given up on . . . just because love calls me to it. And even though I regularly feel that absolutely nothing happens when I sit on my cushion every morning and find my own identity in the Eucharist . . . I know that for me it's about having the heart of an educator . . . and being willing to sit in the middle of the mess and say, "Thank you" and "Help." ◦

> We cultivate a very small field for Christ,
> but we love it, knowing that God does not
> require great achievements,
> but a heart that holds back nothing for self.
>
> —Saint Rose Philippine Duchesne

Praying at 95

Beatrice Brennan, RSCJ

I

To live this long is an amazing grace. One of its unexpected joys is how alive one can feel spiritually as the slow dismantling of other human processes goes on. The Bible speaks of "laughing in the latter day." Prayer, for me, is like that at times. And always, a song of gratitude and joy.

The center of our prayer here at Teresian House, our elder care center in Albany, is the Eucharist. As the wheelchairs and walkers stream into the chapel for Mass, it feels like being in the hungry crowd in Galilee when Jesus fed the multitudes. With them follow all the needy of the world, hungry for bread on every level of human experience.

At other times I pray at my bedroom window, which opens on a tree-rimmed lawn and all of the space beyond. When I sit there looking out, I feel at one with the universe. Crowds join me there from all around the globe. As with Zacchaeus in the tree, I strain for a look at Jesus. I am increasingly aware of not being alone as crowds of people press in at my side. Many are in distress, reaching out with me for answers or comfort or courage to wrestle with huge problems. At other times, sheer wonder wells up deep within, and I join the multitudes of Muslims putting down their prayer rugs when the muezzin cries out that God is great. In short, I never pray alone.

In old age, a remembered word from Scripture or poetry or a precious memory arises as it is needed. One of my favorites is Shakespeare's "Haply I think on Thee." Also, "I would not change my state with kings."

At other times prayer is an earthy groan – one of those unspeakable groanings Paul wrote about in Romans. It is the Spirit groaning in my consciousness when the news is particularly bloody. Images of violence hurl me into the mystery of evil. That, too, lies deep within God's heart, and I just stand as Jesus' mother did as her son was crucified.

In both the lights and darks of a psyche prone to alternating (and sometimes simultaneous) highs and lows, I rock with the paradoxes of reality. It is only God who keeps my little skiff afloat.

At a deeper, quieter level of consciousness runs an undefined awareness of God's presence, similar, I think, to that union of old married couples who may rarely or never put love into words. It has become their life.

So prayer becomes a steady underlying trust bearing me along.

II

At the heart of our Judeo-Christian heritage is the belief that every human being is uniquely known and loved by God. No two of us commune with God in exactly the same way, even when we pray together. What follows is just a sketch of what prayer is like for me.

It is like breathing – something I do without knowing it, though I know when I stop! I breathe in harmony with God's own breathing over our amazing planet – so lovely we are dumbstruck at times. At other times I assert my creaturehood and use the psalmist's words to cry "O God, my God, how wonderful is your name over all the earth." And I know in doing so that God listens to my voice. That sense of God's personal involvement in my prayer is something relatively new. Silent praise wells up without my knowing how, and I get lost in the mystery, like an astronaut in outer space.

III

Chesterton once said that if a thing is worth doing it is worth doing badly. I often think of that when I sit down to pray. My mind and imagination keep darting about even as I hear the spirit say, "Be still and know that I am God." Of late, instead of trying to center down, I follow the dance and find it always leads me to some corner of the real world where God is waiting: a barracks in Afghanistan where a soldier grapples with a demon saying, "end it all," or a room on my corridor where someone tries to remember the way to the dining room.

At such times I remember Jesus saying to Mary Magdalen in the garden, "Do not cling to me. Go tell my brothers and sisters I have risen."

At times, words carry that strong sense of God invading deep caverns in my heart. By now, their number has shrunk down to a handful, loaded with the weight of decades of remembrance. At the end of the noviceship* at Kenwood* at night adoration*: "I to my beloved and my beloved to me."

Prayer was not always as all-inclusive as this. As I look back over many decades I ruefully admit that it was mainly about myself – a cry for love that may have looked to God as very ego-centered, but which patiently turned outward toward the world, and more recently the unknown reaches of a cosmos I don't begin to comprehend.

So in the end I find that prayer in old age is not something I have finally "got right." It is rather "hanging in" and letting God carry on dismantling the castles in the sand I have been building as the tide slides in. "Lord save us, we perish," called Peter in the storm at sea. And the Lord said, "Come," and he walked on water to be near him.

So in my end is my beginning. What lies beyond we know only, "Eye hath not seen." But after a lifetime built on faith, one can want quite happily to be carried out to sea.

Joy

I hold in my depths
all things not yet said.
They are waiting to set free
the joy my mind cannot
claim or contain.
Thought and feeling
have only just begun
to know each other.
One is still too timid
to trust in words;
the other, a child,
too newly born for speech.

— Virginia O'Meara, RSCJ

Heart-Communication

Muriel Cameron, RSCJ

With distress, as a young novice in the Society, I declared to my mistress of novices that I did not know how to pray. She wisely told me that I would never be concerned or wanting to know more about prayer if I were not already praying. She told me that the way to learn to pray was to pray. I took this advice, asking for a deeper gift of prayer, the gift of a heart-knowledge of the love of Jesus. As time went on during the novitiate, I came to realize that my experience of this love was often quietly resting, often without thoughts or insights, but with an interior certainty that I was in Christ, caught in the ambience of the mystery of his love.

Later in my religious formation, the time of preparation for final vows, two unique descriptions of prayer articulated ways of praying. One image was the Chinese symbol for "love," along with the comment that in the Chinese language there is no definitive word for "love" as in English, but rather a description of the experience of love, namely "heart-communication," or "heart-communion," or the sense of silently saying to Christ, "Receive my heart into your heart, and let me receive your heart into mine."

The second lasting explanation of prayer from my year of probation* was called "Walk the dog!" By this is meant: find a psalm, a phrase or a word of Scripture that strikes an inner chord. Return to the passage, let it sink into your heart and lead you to inner silence. If you become distracted, repeat the word again and again. In my later years I find that some of these scriptural words naturally arise in my psyche, helping me return to touchstones of grace or name a current experience.

Besides descriptions of my prayer, I have some foundational convictions that lead me to trust my experience and longings for God. First: desire is the beginning of the gift. The mere fact of one's holy desire is a sign of God's action, coupled with an assurance that God never frustrates good desires. Second: in John's gospel, Jesus tells us, "I will teach you and remind you of all I have said to you." With a hungry heart and desire to learn from Jesus himself, we will be taught by God. Third: in Paul's letter to the Romans we are assured that even when "we cannot choose words to pray properly, the Spirit expresses our plea in a way that could never be put into words, and God, who knows everything in our hearts knows perfectly well what is meant, and that the pleas of the saints expressed by the Spirit are according to the mind of God" (8:26-27). My convictions give me confidence for entering into times of formal prayer. I trust that the time will be blessed, that God's love is gift, not my intellectual effort, and that all I need to do is to be present with an open heart, as a little bird opens its mouth to be fed by the mother bird. Even if tired or distracted, I can "be" and yearn like the little bird.

My times of prayer are not restricted to ritual, or formal times of prayer, but are a dimension of ordinary life, like sending darts of love or pleas for help to pierce the heavens. Sometimes these prayers are utterly simple: thank you, come, help, take care, or simply saying the name of Jesus with confidence and love.

Additional entrances to prayer involve my "symbolic life," such as quietly sitting with a dream, asking the Holy Spirit to unfold its message as I play with the images, feelings and possibilities of the dream. When clarity does not come quickly, I wait patiently in trustful silence, perhaps over a period of time, until the "aha" moment comes, always remembering God's presence in my unconscious which contains treasures of the Spirit.

As I am one captivated by the visual arts, taking time to allow an image to speak and permeate my being leads to inner joy and peace. At times, gazing at a variety of images of the same Scripture passage will draw me into imaginative contemplation. One variance of color, symbol, detail, or a particular setting will call for a resonance with my own spirit so that the Scripture comes alive in a new way, particularly when praying the Gospels. Listening to classical music draws my being into the transcendent realm of God's mysteries.

The liturgy of the Eucharist is significant prayer for me. To avoid distraction and to participate meaningfully, I practice deep listening, which links the words and symbols with the concrete realities of my personal life and my awareness of the needs of the world. Long ago, pondering Pierre Teilhard de Chardin's essay on the Eucharist in *Hymn of the Universe* imprinted a sense of the cosmic Christ's presence in this sacramental celebration. I call to mind Teilhard's articulations on the sense of the fire, intimacy and energy of Christ's love, which are celebrated. The moment of the offertory brings me close to all whom I love as I recall Teilhard's prayer for the offering: "One by one, Lord, I see and I love all those you have given me to sustain and charm my life." When I am separated and yearn for a closeness to those I love, I find consolation during this moment of the eucharistic celebration.

Spiritual reading and striving to become increasingly familiar with the Scriptures, both by daily reading and, when possible, attentive study, contribute to the richness of my formal prayer.

And lastly, my interior life and prayer are nurtured by contemplative practices leading to inner silence and mindfulness. These practices sharpen my senses of gratitude, of joyful delight, of compassion, of wonder, of amazement at the work of God in the tiniest details of life, even in periods of struggle. I am reminded that "Nothing can separate us from the love of God" (Romans 8:35). ∽

Just Showing Up

Maureen J. Chicoine, RSCJ

Prayer for me is a place and time where I can be totally free, totally myself. I feel welcome and at home. It usually leaves me with a deep sense of gratitude just for "being."

I didn't always feel this way. I was introduced to the basics of meditation and prayer as a teenager in Sodality* in high school. When I entered religious life, I was exposed to a discursive form of meditation and a rigid time and place to pray, usually in a chapel. Not a morning person, I showed up and usually slept through the early prayer time, awakened only by my companions' sudden movements and coughs.

It was not until I was in my late twenties and the reforms of religious life that Vatican II introduced, that I was able to pray in a way that was more conducive to spiritual growth. Early on I developed a way of praying: usually alone in my room or outside, with a cup of coffee, favorite icon/s, and music. It was still in the morning, but usually not at the crack of dawn. Using music developed accidently – first as an easy way to time my prayer and screen out distractions. Later it became integral to the prayer atmosphere. A book on prayer by the husband and wife team of Anne and Barry Ulanov, *Primary Speech: a Psychology of Prayer*, was formative in helping me develop a style of prayer that suited my personality. I used the book's excellent resources listed in its appendix. I periodically reread it and marvel at their insights.

Throughout my life, I have been blessed with a series of excellent spiritual directors, who have enabled me to develop this freedom in prayer. They have guided me at key moments of discernment in which I have found a real deepening of the sense of gratitude and freedom. Spiritual reading outside of prayer time has been a way to grow. I have reveled in the insights of Teresa of Avila, John of the Cross, Julian of Norwich and Ignatius of Loyola. I am fascinated by the area where science and theology intersect, especially in the work of Pierre Teilhard de Chardin and his modern interpreters such as Ilia Delio.

I think I would call my method of prayer *lectio divina** with sound and image. I tend to be "heady," so in prayer I like to use other senses – sound, touch, taste, sight. I start with the readings of the day and enjoy the format of *Give Us This Day.** Between the psalms, readings and biography of the day, I usually find some nugget of inspiration.

Over the years, poets such as T.S. Eliot, Thomas Merton, Wendell Barry, John Kavanagh, Mary Oliver and Caryl Houselander have provided words to savor. Not that I don't have days of just dry showing up – and my mind is often like a lively gray squirrel leaping from branch to branch. But for me the experience is a *gestalt* – a sense of being on the edge of infinite mystery. Chasing, reaching out to what Karl Rahner calls the "infinitely receding horizon of being." Whatever, whoever is the Divine Other simply boggles my mind and calls me to go deeper.

I love to pray outdoors, but that is not always possible, so I try to have a "patch of blue," a glimpse of the sky in my frame of vision. On retreat, when I often don't use music, I love to be outside and listen to the sounds around me and savor the sights that being in nature brings.

The music, originally a way to time my prayer without looking at a clock, has become the playlist of my prayer. I find choral music, especially unaccompanied, lifts my heart. I resonate with the sound of Eastern Rite liturgical music, especially Russian, Taizé, Native American flute and Celtic music, especially the pipes and unaccompanied Irish *Sean nós*, or old-style singing. Mostly the words are not important, but occasionally a song will become almost a theme of prayer – and those songs range from religious to secular to traditional.

Images are very important. I am especially fond of Rublev's icon of the Trinity, which has been a constant presence in my prayer corner since the 1970s. Other icons come and go as well as images from all different kinds of sources – art, newspapers, magazines and the internet. *Lectio divina** with images has been a way to connect without thought. I have used artists such as Monet and Chagall, and modern works such as Nava's tapestry, the *Baptism of Christ*, in the Los Angeles Cathedral. But images can also come from films such as *Of Gods and Men*, *The Mission* or *Godspell*. The soundtrack from films such as these and others have also accompanied my prayer.

When I had a very active ministry as a parish leader, the prayer and the ministry did a kind of counterpoint dance with each feeding into and nourishing the other. Now that my ministry is less intense, I am hopeful that will still continue as I work with young adults and have more time and space for enriching my prayer. Every now and then, persons from past or present will leap vividly into my prayer, and I try to envelop them in the prayer time – without knowing why they have come to mind. My prayer corner has a little red book that has names of people who have asked me to pray for them or for whom I feel a responsibility to pray.

I can honestly say I enjoy and look forward to having a daily time of prayer and extended times during retreat. What would I say to a beginner about prayer? Just be yourself and be free – there are no rules except to show up. ~

A Litany of Symbols to the Heart of Jesus

O Sleeping Beauty
  wreathed in blossoming thorn
On Trellis – Transom – Tree:
  awaken me.

O Ripened Fruit
  redgoldleafed by the sun,
You Apple of my I:
  my hunger satisfy.

O Tented Arc
  in shadowed dark of noon:
Your Tabernacle set
  where our hearts met.

O Cup of Wine
  Your Vine pours out on earth:
My grapes of wrath O press
  to blood you bless.

O Water, salty Flood
  where Spirit broods:
Over my primal sea
  speak your: "Let be,"

O Setting Sun, whose rise
  my westering eyes saw not:
Be now my Orient
  Easter my Lent.

O Final Firebird,
  Phoenix of rebirth:
Inflame my frosty stone
  Of blood, heart, bone.

O Cosmic Dancer,
  Resting when the lance
Rent the veiled Temple:
  Draw me to your dance.

O Endless Carol,
  final Crown of Song,
Wedding Circlet,
  weaving stars among,

O Heart, red Rose and Wreath,
  still Center of the Wheel,
O failing Breath,
  O Thread upon the Reel,

O Love and Lotus,
  Mandala to hold
Was, Is, and Will be:
  Perfect Rose of Gold,

Embrace, encircle,
  nest and foster me
  while time spins on,
Till our Death sets me free
  Eternally.

—Madeleine Sophie Cooney, RSCJ

Passive Contemplation

Theresa Mei-fen Chu, RSCJ

During the past twenty years, I have followed a simple way of prayer called passive contemplation. I learned it from John Govan, SJ, in 1993. I set aside one hour each morning, usually making it the first thing I do. I cherish the moment when, outside the windows, it is still dark. I follow four steps:

1. Putting myself in the loving presence of God;

2. Asking for the grace to die to myself;

3. Waiting like a servant, being ready to follow no other lead but that of the Lord himself;

4. Short expressions of love to one of the three persons, the Father, or the Son or the Holy Spirit.

These four steps are equally important to me, though they are not equal in lengths. The first two and the last steps are usually short. The bulk of the time is spent in the darkness of waiting.

In the first step, I try to put the accent on God loving me. Often, I need to repeat to myself a number of times that I am in the loving presence of God so that it is not just a formula I say. Once I am aware of it, I move on to the petition.

I ask for no other grace except that of dying to myself. I try not to elaborate on the petition in order to avoid giving God hints how this might be done, but simply stating the desire in all sincerity. I am not afraid to emphasize this wish, being aware that I truly need it.

For the third step, I do not use any text, not even the Bible. Neither do I admit my own thoughts or anyone else's to guide me, no matter how helpful they may seem to be. I only accept gratefully the lead of God if it comes. Usually, I wait in darkness, but waiting is never in vain, I know.

Once I asked my director how I would know whether a thought comes from God or from elsewhere. His answer was: "You would know." Good thoughts have come to me often, but I do not dwell on them because I clearly know they originate from my own store of memory. I gently return to the darkness where my loving God is present, and I continue to wait.

Distractions crowd into the darkness. Once I become aware, however, I cash in on this weakness and acknowledge before God that I am a mortal human being. My director told me not to let myself be upset by distractions. He used the example of the waiting area at a train station. "You are waiting for your train, but while so doing, you can't help noticing people around you," he said. So when this happens, I just resume my post as a waiting servant. It is important not to look at my watch, although for years I did it every day, always at forty minutes after the beginning! In fact, looking at my watch only makes the hour seem longer. Be it easy or difficult, I try to be faithful to the hour because I believe that making it non-negotiable is my way to acknowledge God's absolute right over me; and by the same token, for me to stay in touch with my foundation: I am a creature, a child of God and a loved sinner.

I have found this method of prayer good because vis-à-vis God and neighbor, it is putting me, inch by inch, in the place where I belong. It has taken from me some unnecessary tension. In the past twenty years, life has become brighter, happier and more enjoyable all around.

This method goes hand in hand with the examen* of consciousness every night. That, too, I find helpful, although I tend to slip back to the old way of examining myself. Instead of posing as judge over myself, I now try to go over the day with Jesus, letting the events of the day slowly roll down one after another. While in the presence of Jesus, I pay attention to my heart's reaction to each, whether I felt peaceful or otherwise. Then I talk to Jesus about it, either thanking him or asking his pardon. It is always an effort for me, but the fifteen minutes usually pass very quickly.

Prayer has its unique importance for me. I came through some turbulent periods in my life before I learned this method of prayer. But I have held on to the formula of one hour every morning, the importance of which had been impressed on me long ago during my noviceship*. I have held on to this structure no matter how unsatisfactory prayer itself seems to me during times of difficulty. I believe that a house needs to be built on rock, and prayer is that structural rock of the edifice of my life. ∽

Prayer in the Face of Incomprehensible Violence

Maria Cimperman, RSCJ

In prayer we come to Jesus,
with everything that touches our life,
with the sufferings and hopes of humanity.
We learn to remain in silence
and poverty of heart before Him.

—Constitutions §20

What do you do when something happens you cannot even begin to understand? When words at some point fail? When figuring it out cannot answer the absence? On July 17, 2014, Malaysian Flight 17 was shot down over the Ukraine. Sister Phil Tiernan, a Religious of the Sacred Heart from Australia, was on that flight. I had met Phil only a few weeks earlier at the Janet Erskine Stuart Centenary Conference in England. The following are excerpts from seven Facebook entries in the days that followed her death.

July 20, 2014

I wept when I heard Phil was on the plane that was shot down. My heart is sad, broken. And now she is teaching me about the Sacred Heart of Jesus, who loved greatly and fully and whose heart is one with the wounded heart of humanity and the wounded earth. I am heading off to Sunday liturgy shortly, and I keep hearing: "this is my body, this is my blood, given for you," given in love, given now over a war-torn and bloodied landscape with the blood from the world on it.

Phil lived our call and invitation to discover and reveal God's love. She is not done. Phil is inviting us all ... and so is our God who loves and weeps with us. We are being called.

July 21, 2014

As my heart breaks with the violence that causes such pain, Phil calls me to relationship with all the people on the plane, with their families, co-workers and friends. I am now also connected, intertwined with those who planned, built, positioned and launched the missile that shot the plane and people out of the sky on July 17. Our lives are now inextricably linked . . . and I do not know what to do with that right now . . . I need not know right now. Yet Phil is challenging me.

Phil is widening my heart and our hearts to the entire world . . . as Jesus did and does . . . beyond my understanding . . . and calling us . . . as Jesus does. We are being called. And I pray to be open(ed) . . .

July 22, 2014

We are in the midst of the paschal mystery and I cannot yet see . . . I am straining to hear the notes, to see and understand the gestures all around, to watch carefully.

I know Phil, who planned for an ordinary flight back to beloved family, friends and community, is offering us an extraordinary call. Not one she would have chosen, I am certain, for she knew her own share of suffering and would not want to be a source of suffering. But she is taking us with her on this extraordinary, albeit unwanted path . . . and I know she is calling us forth. I sense her taking my hand to keep me going.

I am trying to listen keenly, watch attentively. I see her piercing blue eyes. She wants us to see more, to hear more. She wants us to see bigger and wider than herself. She has my attention.

I don't want to miss a movement, a gesture, a sound. I want to hear what is being said beneath the words, gestures. I want to respond. And so I pray to have my eyes, ears, heart and arms open.

July 27, 2014

I know – actually, I believe – that even as I grieve and miss people who die, they are united in God. I believe that somehow that Oneness in God, that All of God, holds all. God, who is Love, holds all in love.

But death is still not easy, at least not for me . . . so what might Phil be offering me, us? During the Stuart Conference, we recalled words of Janet Erskine Stuart: "If we love well and much, we shall need no other preparation for death; squandering ourselves and what we have on God and on our neighbor, that is the best way to prepare for it."

I was caught by that quote then and ever more so now. It's not about focusing on death, is it? It's about loving now. Phil indeed loved well and much. I have more than once reflected that she is calling forth the best in me.

I have also been pondering "give your death away." Ronald Rolheiser, OMI, has spoken about one of the tasks at the end of the second half of life as giving your death away. Perhaps Phil is helping me understand a bit more. In one sense we all want to give our lives away – in love. People do that in marriage, as they raise children, as they care for one another. In religious life, our profession and living of vows speaks of this. Phil gave her life away – to love, to serve. Phil is now also giving her death away. Her death is calling us just as her life did – to our best.

Her death will teach me, if I am willing to look at what happened in the Ukraine, to see how it is connected to the larger violence around us and near us, including in my city, Chicago, and to find a response that is not the revenge reflex too often present. The consummate educator, Phil is trying to teach, offering herself, calling us to more. She, too, is like the grain of wheat that fell to the ground and died. What new life, what needed response, is invited to grow in me, in us? She invited us, as Jesus invites us ... and while I do not sense this journey will be either quick or easy, as I look at the world around us, battered and yet full of so much possibility, it is abundantly clear another way has to grow, has to bear fruit.

So in life, let us "love well and much ... squandering ourselves and what we have on God and on our neighbor ..." I pray to love like this ... I pray to be open ...

July 31, 2014

Of course we lament. We lament because we hope. If we had no hope we would simply despair. *The Book of Lamentations* is so powerful precisely because of this. So we lament lives tragically lost because people shot a missile at other people. On this level it doesn't matter if the particular people on Flight 17 were not the intended victims. How do we even measure life with such intent?

Because something in us realizes this is wrong, deeply wrong, we lament. We lament the loss of life in in the Middle East, in the Ukraine, in the Congo, in Brazil and more. We lament the deaths to violence of so many young people in Chicago. We lament because we hope for so much more. We believe in a vision far deeper, wider and fuller than what we see.

Yet lament is dangerous. It is dangerous because it is rooted in hope, rooted in a vision of God's way of life that seeks to love, to serve, to maximize potential for the good of all of creation. We know so much more is possible. And because we know this we will discern. We will read this reality with mind and heart, and probe what it is saying, what Phil and so many others are saying. And a response will come forth.

In our *Constitutions* we say "Rooted in Christ through contemplation we wish to be women who create communion." (§6) I have always found that both welcoming and challenging. Create communion. Phil created communion among those she met. Now she has met a missile . . . and she keeps reminding me that there are people in every part of this. Missiles are made by people. Hatred and discord are made by people. Mercy and peace are also made by people. Reconciliation and peace-building are also made by people. God is in the midst of them all, yes. Grace is needed in this. God's grace is abundant . . . if we desire it.

This is exactly where we are being called to be people who create communion:

> By the witness of our love and apostolic dedication,
> by sharing the life of our peoples
> whose cultures are rich and varied,
> our communities throughout the world
> help to further communion in Christ. (§6).

Communion in Christ . . . a Christ who loves, not counting the cost. A Christ who said, "Feed my sheep, tend my lambs." A Christ who also said we will not do this alone: "Receive my Spirit."

In the Society of the Sacred Heart we talk about the need for our lives to be "wholly contemplative, wholly apostolic." Each one is absolutely necessary. I long for my God, and I have in the past days of reflection often prayed to be open. "The Spirit dwelling within us gradually transforms us . . ." (§21) I pray to be transformed ever more into God's likeness of love needed for this time. I shall pray for all of us, too. Being "wholly apostolic" includes that.

> Caught up as we are in the desires of His Heart,
> we want people to grow in dignity, as human beings
> and as children of God.
> Our starting point is the Gospel,
> with all that it demands from us of love, forgiveness
> and justice,
> and of solidarity with those who are poor
> and rejected by the world. (§7)

Phil is calling us. The world is calling us, each and all. God is calling us. So we pray to be open and to respond. ∼

Gazing on the Beloved

Lillian Conaghan, RSCJ

How does a 91-year old resident at Oakwood* pray? I will tell you my simple story. If I were closer to being a mystic, it would be more interesting, but the truth will set me free.

We have the privilege of daily Eucharist. I prepare for that great prayer of thanksgiving by a pattern of prayer called *lectio divina*,* a pattern that includes reading the sacred text slowly and savoring it, pondering a word or phrase that has touched my heart, and letting the text lead me to prayer and dialogue with God. The readings of Mass call me to walk with Jesus in a special way each day, and sometimes a surprising insight is found in the opening prayer of the liturgy.

We have additional help here at Oakwood to strengthen us on our journey to the Father, that is, the availability of many spiritual directors.

It is springtime as I write, a time of invitation to linger while walking through the gardens. The American Beauty rose mirrors the depth of God's love for me. The peach rose gives permanence to the afternoon sunset. The stately calla lily receives mixed reviews of adoration and detestation. Genesis seems to have been written as I walk with my Creator through so much beauty, and sigh, "It is truly very good."

There are days when the desire to adore, to praise God, to beg to know more deeply the Heart of Jesus does not come easily. Then I try reading from Nan Merrill's translation of the psalms, *Psalms for Praying: An Invitation to Wholeness*, especially psalms 86 and 92.

During a time of transition, moving from St. Louis to Atherton, California, psalm 86 helped me remain in touch with my Beloved:

> *Be present to me and receive my prayer;*
> *imbue me with strength, and*
> *help me to release each fear.*

Then psalm 92 helped me to express my gratitude for the place where I had been sent:

It is good to give thanks to You,
O Beloved,
to sing praises to your Holy Name,
To affirm your steadfast love
in the morning,
and your faithfulness through
the night,
To the music of the spheres,
to the melody of the universe!
For You, Heart of my heart, gladden
my soul,
as I proclaim with joy the harmony
and beauty of creation.

There is still another way to pray and that is to visit our sisters confined to wheelchairs or their rooms. You often see the face of God. ∼

God Intrusions

Margaret Conroy, RSCJ

The way of prayer I find best is to sit on a cushion in our community chapel before the tabernacle, look at the readings for the day and zero in on any word or image that speaks to me. My mind never becomes empty, alas, and all kinds of thoughts chase each other around my head, but when I have an image – water, fire, light, road, mountain, jar, cloud, friend – I can center on that and it reveals the Lord to me. My favored image is the tree planted beside a stream of living water, drawing up God's life or love or grace in order to grow, stay green, bear flowers and fruits constantly, provide shelter for the birds and a shade for all God's creatures.

My prayer time is very early, when all is quiet and dark except for our little chapel. It is linked to daily Mass, when each day I ask the Father to say to me, "You are my child; today I beget you," so that for that day, at least, I love with Christ's heart and see with his eyes, hear with his ears, think with his mind, decide with his will and speak his words.

These are the deepest, most significant moments of my day, and they are part of the fabric of my life. God leaves me as self-centered as ever, but I do experience peace, deep contentment and trust that God will give me the grace I need for whatever the future holds.

What I want from prayer is to be taken over completely by the Lord so that he is the one my presence gives to others. I cannot do much anymore because of deafness and arthritis, and I am not an extrovert, but I hope my presence makes God present somehow to the people I meet and with whom I interact – the prisoners, women with AIDS, their children and those who work with them, my own little community and our friends.

What do I personally think prayer is? Well, essentially, presence, awareness (subliminal often, but not far from the surface) of God, in my case, mostly of Christ. I don't know whether faith or awareness comes first. For me, God intruded on my life when I was very young and has always been near, so I have never doubted God's existence or goodness. The world, especially the world of nature, is full of revelations of God for me.

What would I say to a beginner about prayer? Make personal prayer, generously given, a habit, a daily commitment. God will not be outdone in generosity. And do not abandon the Eucharist, which is food for us on our journey to God, with God. ∾

When you come from the altar, bring not the ashes, but the fire.

—Saint Rose Philippine Duchesne

Recognizing God's Presence

Trudy Considine, RSCJ

Prayer is being with God. Through this grace God unites us with the whole of the cosmos, the body of Christ. Prayer is a place of growth and learning. Prayer is what God does within me. It can be secret and hidden, and I don't know what happens, but God leaves me in quiet and peace.

Prayer can be journaling through a hard time or talking things through with the Lord until peace comes. God can be seen in other people's actions.

Nature is prayer revealing God's Presence, especially birds singing like the cardinals or yellow wing blackbirds, or cocker spaniels, golden retrievers or cute terriers who come looking for friendship, or extraordinary blossoms or majestic trees. God is the space between leaves.

God is everywhere expressed so my recognizing God's Presence is prayer. ∽

An Affair of the Heart

Suzanne Cooke, RSCJ

Years ago I learned that Saint Madeleine Sophie spoke of prayer in terms of a conversation. She spoke and God listened, and then God spoke and she listened. I believe prayer is essentially a relationship, and like all relationships, prayer begins in the silence of one's heart.

Consider any relationship. Its beginning is a spark or an attraction to the other, first experienced in the silence of our mind and heart. This instinct urges us to seek out the other, to come to know the other. This relationship can only grow into a friendship if this initial attraction or intuition is attended to or nurtured. One listens in silence. One spends time with the other, listening and learning. This listening engages one's heart and mind, one's entire being or soul. Eventually the listening blossoms into dialogue. One becomes so engaged by the other that listening and dialogue become effortless. The mutual engagement of hearts and minds of the two involved in the relationship leads to intimacy, to genuine love. Such love is communion. The communion is dynamic; therefore, silence is constant if one is to continue to learn about and from the other. Prayer is an affair of the heart; it is an act of friendship.

Friendship

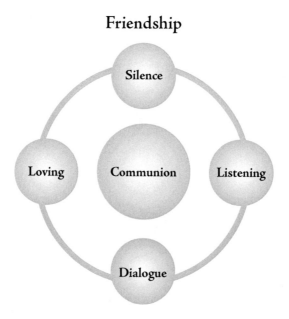

Mother Stuart* encouraged RSCJs to live absorbed in God's interests. She described prayer as breathing. "Prayer is the aspiration, the breathing of the soul," she wrote. "It is our unexpressed desire for union. It is any turning of the mind and heart to God." She saw our lives as RSCJs as the "inward spirit of consecration which has two movements, like the vital act of breathing, and the outward and inward movements are each incomplete without the other. The deep intake of breath is given back again as the sound of a voice, carrying its gift from God."

Live Absorbed In God's Interests

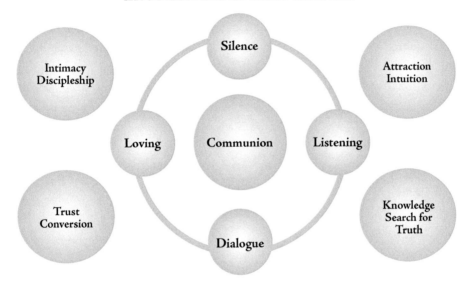

The longer I am a Religious of the Sacred Heart, the more deeply I believe that *silence* is the essential context for prayer. At the 2008 General Chapter,* we said:

> *In the secret place of the heart the Spirit gradually*
> *transforms our feelings and responses, and draws us into*
> *an intimate relationship with God. The Spirit attunes*
> *us to the heartbeat of our people to discover the presence*
> *and love of God in everyday life. When we contemplate*
> *the Heart of Christ we enter into the movement of the*
> *Spirit who develops in us a listening heart.*

How do we develop listening hearts? I think it is essential to view *time* as the opportunity to know Christ. If our action is to be permeated with the presence of God, then we must find time to listen to the Spirit dwelling within our hearts. It is Christ's Spirit that urges and beckons us forward. The only way to satisfy this internal urgency to know Christ is to decide to spend time with him, to take time to read and listen to the Scriptures, and to use time to learn of Jesus from others. Such investment of self in listening leads to knowledge of Christ. To come to know Christ is to discover the Father. One grows in knowledge of Christ by trusting the Spirit within. In other words, the Spirit leads us to Christ who points us to God. Living in communion with the fullness of God is the ultimate fruit of our friendship with Christ.

Each of us uses *time* differently. We have a great richness in our tradition as RSCJs. Practices like centering prayer,* *lectio divina,* * and the examen* help us to refine our attentiveness and listening so that we can find Christ in all things. Praying with the Constitutions* and chapter documents* strengthens our *cor unum** and inspires us to realize Saint Madeleine Sophie's vision by engaging fully in the Society's mission.

Live Absorbed In God's Interests

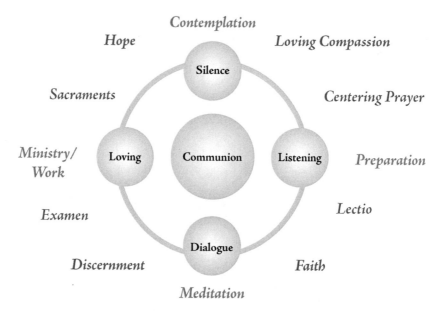

One Heart, One Mind in Jesus Christ

Prayer as the Interior Life

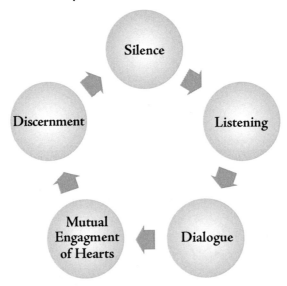

Time engaged in prayer, both meditation and contemplation, bears fruit in our action as it is our expression of loving compassion. Participation in the sacraments nourishes our spirit so we can better identify the ultimate source of our hope.

I once heard Barbara Bowe, RSCJ, explain that reality for the RSCJ means both our interior life where God's transforming love dwells and the outer world around us where God's daily revelation and mysterious presence in people and events summons us to apostolic zeal. Breathing in and breathing out – that is who we are.

In the end I think of prayer as time with God. Location is immaterial, but the quality of the silence and listening is essential if my friendship with Christ is to deepen. The deeper the silence, the more acute the listening and, in time, the stronger the communion. ∿

My Life Has Given Me Gifts

Dolores Copeland, RSCJ

I cannot imagine not having Christian Meditation* as a part of my daily, ordinary, day by day life. Christian Meditation is simplicity itself, but simple does not mean easy.

My life has given me gifts. If I were asked to state, at this time in my life, my three greatest gifts, I would answer: 1) the gift of my life, 2) the gift of my vocation as an RSCJ, and 3) the gift of knowing Christian Meditation.

Christian Meditation is the prayer of the heart – the prayer of faith. In silence we accept that God knows our needs and will eventually complete us. Learning to be attentive teaches us to be silent. Learning to be silent teaches us to pray. Learning to be silent eventually teaches us to pray as Jesus summons and as Saint Paul calls – pray without ceasing – pray always.

To meditate is to decide to restore a healthy, dynamic balance to life. (Laurence Freeman) The mantra, prayer word or sacred word, is an *ascesis* – not a tool or a technique, but a commitment to a spiritual path and the daily, steady discipline this entails. It is a work of love. It releases a transformative power in us if meditation is part of our life day by day. Every time we sit down to meditate there is a dying and rebirth. The personal, inner change in us as we meditate can be described in what Saint Paul tells us is the harvest of the Spirit: love, joy, peace, patience, kindness, goodness, fidelity, gentleness and self-control. (Galatians 5:5)

One of the joys in my life at present is the possibility I have to teach Christian Meditation to children. Children take to meditation very naturally. They are, by nature, simple. They ask to meditate, they appreciate learning to meditate and they thank me for the opportunity. A sixth grade child said to me. "Thank you for teaching me to meditate. I absolutely love meditation, and I meditate in my room at home. It has really helped me to calm down."

The experience of the practice of meditation becomes the teacher. ∾

A Personal Way of Praying the Rosary

Martha Curry, RSCJ

All of my life I have had a deep devotion to Our Lady. She has been at the center of my life of prayer since I was a child. I am sure that I learned to say the "Hail Mary" at the same time as I learned to say the "Our Father." Also, saying the rosary has been a daily practice of mine since I was in grade school. It simply was part of each day's activities. This practice was reinforced when I entered the Society at Kenwood in the 1950s. At that time, we novices and all RSCJs, every day said "the rosary of rule," even though our Constitutions* never prescribed such an obligation.

Our original Constitutions of 1815, however, did prescribe devotion to Mary. In the fourth paragraph, after declaring that the aim of the Society is "to glorify the Sacred Heart of Jesus," the Constitutions continues, "The Society proposes also to honor with particular devotion the most Holy Heart of Mary, which was so perfectly conformed in everything to the adorable Heart of Jesus her Divine Son." (§ 4. IV) A century and a half later, the Second Vatican Council mandated that all religious orders review and restate their constitutions. Our Constitutions of 1982 rephrased our practice of Marian devotion in these words:

> *Mary, woman of faith among the People of God, lives*
> *close to us, as she does to everything that radiates the*
> *life of her Son. Our Society entrusts itself in a special*
> *way to her whose heart is united and conformed to*
> *that of Jesus, so that she may lead us to Him. (§9)*

Among the other reforms initiated by the Second Vatican Council was a renewed emphasis on the rites of the Church, especially the Mass and, in many people's minds, a de-emphasis on popular devotions, including the recitation of the rosary. I fell prey to this supposed de-emphasis. After the close of the council in 1965, I stopped saying my daily rosary. In a few years' time, however, I realized that my prayer life lacked something. I soon realized that bringing the rosary back into my life was an excellent way to follow the words of our Constitutions, to turn to Mary "so that she may lead us to [Jesus]." I turned to Mary to help me delve into the mysteries of the heart of her son. The whole purpose of praying the rosary is to contemplate the mysteries of the life of Jesus, his joys, sufferings, and final triumph over death.

During the next three decades I said my daily rosary and my closeness to Mary returned. Through my contemplation of the mysteries of the rosary, Mary brought me closer to the concerns of Jesus' heart and, therefore, to the concerns of the world with its sufferings and needs.

However, while I was dutifully praying the Joyful, Sorrowful, and Glorious Mysteries, I became uneasy with three things. First, even though the rosary is designed to help us ponder the life of Jesus, saying the words of the Hail Mary on each bead interfered with my contemplation of these mysteries. I found myself saying the actual words of the Hail Mary less and less. Then I read an article – I can't remember who wrote it or when I read it – that advised saying the Hail Mary only on the first and last bead of each decade. In this new method of saying the rosary, I started hearing other words, the actual words of the mystery proposed. For example, in contemplating the annunciation, the first Joyful Mystery, I would hear most of Gabriel's words and Mary's responses. Or in contemplating Jesus' resurrection, the first Glorious Mystery, the highly evocative words and actions from the gospel readings for Easter week gave me many words and images to ponder.

The second area of unease that I felt in saying the rosary was with the choice of the mysteries themselves. By saying the rosary we are called to contemplate the life of Jesus, but in its original form we go from the time Jesus was twelve years old and lost in the temple to his agony in the garden of Gethsemane. Where are the years of Jesus' teaching, healing, and ministries of his public life? Yes, our Lord's public ministry had been passed over. Then Pope John Paul II, toward the end of his pontificate, proposed adding to the rosary the mysteries of Jesus' public life, which he called the Mysteries of Light: Jesus' baptism, the wedding feast of Cana, Jesus' mission of preaching and healing, the transfiguration, and the Last Supper.

Moving on to the Sorrowful Mysteries brought me to the third area of unease with the recitation of the rosary. As I prayed the rosary for many years, I had to rearrange the Sorrowful Mysteries. As the Sorrowful Mysteries were first designed, again, too much was left out. How can we omit pondering Jesus' betrayal by Judas, his arrest, the denial by Peter, and his sentencing to death by Pilate? Why rush from Gethsemane to what was actually the beginning of his execution: the scourging at the pillar, the crowning with thorns, and the carrying of the cross? So my personal Sorrowful Mysteries are: the agony in the garden, the betrayal by Judas, Jesus being sentenced to death, the scourging and the way of the cross, and the crucifixion.

After contemplating the Sorrowful Mysteries, we move to the Glorious Mysteries: the resurrection, ascension, descent of the Holy Spirit at Pentecost, the assumption of Mary into heaven and the crowning of Mary as Queen of Heaven. The last two of these Glorious Mysteries are the only mysteries not based on actual events recorded in the gospels. So again I adjusted my contemplation while fingering the beads of these last two decades. I turned outside of the gospel accounts, first to the devotion of the Eastern Church called the Dormition of Mary, her falling asleep or death. Realizing that Mary's death preceded her assumption, contemplating the fourth Glorious Mystery gives me the opportunity to call to mind not only Mary's death but also the deaths of so many loved ones. In the company of our Blessed Mother I praise them, thank them for all their gifts to me and love them in new ways. Contemplating this mystery also is an occasion for me to pray for those near death, that their deaths may be a peaceful falling asleep in God.

Finally, my prayer for the last mystery of the rosary is a contemplation of the mystery of the communion of saints. Mary, Queen of Heaven, stands at the head of all of us united in one great community. The last Glorious Mystery gives me an opportunity to give thanks for the blessings of belonging to the community of saints, the community of all the living who participate in the holiness of God. It also gives me the opportunity to realize that not only we humans, but all of nature, participate in the holiness of God, the creator of all. I typically say the rosary at the end of the day, right before I go to sleep; and I pray the Glorious Mysteries on Sunday, the beginning of a new week. How wonderful to begin a new week by pondering my place in the communion of saints. What a wonderful way to end each day by pondering the life of Jesus, and to begin each week with a great prayer of praise and gratitude. ∼

In welcoming God's word
Mary gave Christ to the world.
In receiving the life of Jesus
we give ourselves with Him so that all may have life.

—Constitutions of the Society of the Sacred Heart §22

Anchored in the Word

Kathleen Dolan, RSCJ

In the Gospel
through His words, His attitudes,
His relationship with people,
His way of relating to all created things,
we discover His Heart
wholly given to the Father and all people.

—Constitutions §19

Since my mind tends to wander, I use the readings of the day as the basis for my prayer. Scripture, especially the gospels, provides me with a road map for growing in a deeper knowledge of Jesus and understanding of his ways. Without fail, there is a word, phrase or image that will draw me into deeper conversation and contemplation. The words of the readings are a source of life, energy and, more often than not, a challenge for me. ∾

More than ever let us draw close to the open Heart
of Jesus. Let us meditate on his love, his charity
toward all, and in our turn, may we try to bring
this wherever we have any influence.

—Saint Madeleine Sophie Barat

Waiting on God

Jan Dunn, RSCJ

During my annual retreat,* at some point I usually decide that I will try new ways of praying. I think about trying a theme like focusing on Jesus as healer or praying the "Do not be afraid" passages in Scripture. Or I play with the idea of using art – pictures of the annunciation, the Good Shepherd, or the Sacred Heart – as the springboard for my morning prayer. I think of using music as a way to encounter God. When the weather is lovely in the fall or spring, I play with the idea of walking my prayer. I journal often to get my thoughts out of my head and to trace the ups and downs of my journey.

However, no matter what methods I might experiment with, I always return to the way I am most comfortable being before God each morning before my day begins. I get a cup of coffee, light a candle and return to my bed. I sit upright and open the Scripture readings for the Mass of the day. Then I wait on God! It is as simple as that!

Some days, I am peaceful and quiet. Some mornings I am agitated and noisy. Often the time flies by, but some days it drags and I have to force myself just to stay and "put in the time." Most mornings, now that I live in St. Charles, I watch the sun shed its rays over ground where Philippine* walked and she herself prayed. Remembering her, her companions and her great friend Sophie* centers me for my day and my ministry.

As a young nun, I discovered a prayer by Michel Quoist which describes best how I pray:

> To be here before you, Lord,
> that's all:
> to shut the eyes of my body,
> to shut the eyes of my soul,
> and be still and silent,
> to expose myself to you who are here, exposed to me.
> to be here before you,
> the Eternal Presence . . .

To be before God, bringing my world and everyone in it with me, and to let God work is my way of encountering God. ❧

Sometimes and Always

Mary Ann (Sis) Flynn, RSCJ

I thought it would be simple to write about my prayer but discover it nearly impossible to find the words to express what I hope to convey. Do you ask others how they breathe? Then someone suggested that I offer my reflections as an RSCJ educator, in case my thoughts might be helpful to someone else. It is in this spirit that I speak of "my" prayer.

Throughout my religious life I have studied and practiced many prayer forms, have been introduced to different schools of spirituality, befriended several of the great teachers of prayer in my reading and experience. It is overwhelming to review the opportunities for growth I have been given. So I can say that I pray in different ways at different times depending on the liturgical season, the "season" of my own life, and the particular circumstances of any given day. The desire to learn to "pray always" has led me to experience prayer in many ways.

I – Sometimes

Sometimes I pray in **gratitude**. Waking in the morning to the song of the first bird at daybreak, I thank God for another day of life. Gratitude is a huge part of prayer; gratefulness helps me abide in the divine presence. Gratitude keeps me mindful of all that I have been given. And it is not only thanking for what I have received from God; it is making a return. It is the mutual exchange of love: "I to my beloved and my beloved to me" (Song of Songs 2:16).

I think of Our Lady as the one who has made this full return. Her *Magnificat* tells of her total openness to the divine mystery and I learn from her that prayer is a relationship, a relationship of love. The poet Marie Howe has expressed in her poem the overwhelming power of this realization of being drawn by the Divine:

Annunciation

Even if I don't see it again — nor ever feel it
I know it is — and that if once it hailed me
it ever does —
And so it is myself I want to turn in that direction
not as towards a place, but it was a tilting
within myself,
as one turns a mirror to flash the light to where
it isn't — I was blinded like that — and swam
in what shone at me
only able to endure it by being no one and so
specifically myself I thought I'd die
from being loved like that.

—from *The Kingdom of Ordinary Time*

This experience of being invaded by God is transformative to my prayer and to my relationship to all of life. I believe Saint Madeleine Sophie,* too, knew this world, and I frequently turn to her to be my companion in prayer, because it is clinging to the belief that "being loved like that" is what informs all of life, gives it meaning and joy.

Sometimes the **liturgy**, rich in Scripture texts, guides my prayer. It is the solid basis for my prayer. It is this greater prayer of the church that makes my prayer universal — confirming that my prayer, though deeply personal, is not really mine, but part of, and one with, the Body of Christ and the communion of saints. I love, too, the writings of our mystics and the writings and spiritualities of other traditions — Jewish, Hindu, Buddhist, Muslim and Native American — as well as numerous poets. These inspire me in my desire for union with the divine. And, of course, it is the gospels that reveal the Heart of Jesus, who is the one praying within me for all of creation.

Sometimes it is **nature** that feeds my prayer. Certainly God's creation speaks of the creator. The symbolism and imagery that come from contemplation of nature become prayer and tell us what they know of God. The trees, flowers, birds, the ocean, mountains and stars become sacramental, inspiring us to find the God who is beyond us very present in the daily incarnational reality of our lives. I think often, praying with this awareness, of the oneness and connectedness of all things. Janet Erskine Stuart, RSCJ,* was so gifted in drawing lessons from nature. Her writings and reflections are part of her legacy to us, and I find her reflections practical and beautiful.

Sometimes there is deep **longing**, a sense akin to loneliness, when I know my own smallness. It is time to befriend the night and darkness when I am drawn into the mystery and the deep silence. In the dark, seeds grow deep underground. In the dark, the vastness of the sky and stars appear. Night is the time for lovers. It seems the most truthful time to be just myself, happy to be with God. When this darkness seems difficult, it is still a sacred time. When this night is long, something Thomas Merton wrote resonates: "If you descend into the depths of your own spirit … And arrive somewhere near the center of what you are, you are confronted with the inescapable truth that, at the very roots of your existence you are in immediate and constant contact with the infinite God." (*Palace of Nowhere*, 35)

Sometimes the way I pray is simply **intercession**. When I say I will pray for someone or someone asks for prayer, I respond. I used to recite prayers for them, maybe recite the rosary. Now I bring the intention, the person, the situation into my own thought and take it to God. When I cannot sleep, I find myself remembering situations and people in many parts of the world, especially where there is suffering and need or where I have lived and know people. I feel as though I am praying as did Philippine,* keeping vigil with others, picturing or imagining or remembering them. I even continue my vigil here at Oakwood,* where I live, praying for the sisters who are ill or distressed, asking that they be comforted and strengthened. It is then that I know, too, that others are praying for me, and I feel the one heart we share.

Two practices I have found valuable to a sincere life of prayer are journaling and some form of the examen.* Journaling helps me know my own experience, and checking my consciousness with the examen allows me to review my behavior and motives. It can be humbling, but throws me on God, trying to be really honest … then letting go of even needing to "try"!

II – Always

I have mentioned how I pray sometimes in different ways. I am happy that I have felt free to experience different ways to pray. And I do think there are a few aspects of prayer to which I would say always.

Always it is God who initiates prayer. We are created Godward. There is a longing in us that Love has planted. In chapter 55, the prophet Isaiah speaks of the word spoken forth from the mouth of God, returning to God, having fulfilled its destiny. I was given a glimpse into God's dream for creation in the words of the Japanese poet, Jukichi Yagi:

> *The seed of prayer is sown in heaven.*
> *It pushes its stem toward the earth*
> *and comes to grow there.*
> *It produces an abundance of fruit.*
> *Then, as it becomes seed once more,*
> *it thrusts its way back to heaven.*

Always, I think it's important to know that my prayer is not really only mine. Because it is part of all that I have met, I belong to everyone and I am part of all humanity and there's nothing separate when I pray. I am praying with everybody who is praying at the same time anywhere in the world. United to the divine, I am one with everything. Of course, it is in faith through the Spirit praying in us that this occurs. It is encouraging at this time in my life when active ministry is less. As *The Cloud of Unknowing* declares:

> One loving blind desire for God is more valuable in
> itself, more pleasing to God . . . more beneficial to
> your own growth and more helpful to your friends,
> both living and dead, than anything else you could
> do.

Always, the beauty of God fills everything. The nearness and the mystery of the divine have attracted me all of my life. I believe that one day all comes together in the allness of God and the unity of all in God. Words of Jessica Powers sustain me in my hope to live and to die in that presence:

> When I think of the love of God I become aware
> of my own emptiness of heart. When I think of the
> goodness of God I recall my innumerable needs.
> When I think of the mercy of God I remember
> my own failures. But when I think of the beauty
> of God I cease to exist at all. I become a living
> adoration. ❧

"It is no longer I who live, but Christ who lives in me."

Mary Frohlich, RSCJ

"It is no longer I who live, but Christ who lives in me" (Galatians 2:20). That is my ideal of prayer. In my best moments of deep openness, I know that Christ truly flows in and through me. However, I would be a hypocrite if I suggested that this is what prayer is like all the time. When I was young, I thought that with maturity, the interior life would become calm, integrated and spacious. Instead, it seems as if the interior seas have become rougher with age, frequently upending me in the most humiliating ways. There are days when my prayer is truly desperate. Whether overwhelmed by the demands of ministry or on my knees after an emotional meltdown, I can only surrender myself to the mercy of God.

As for my daily routine of prayer, I usually go to the chapel for thirty to forty-five minutes in the morning before work and about ten to thirty minutes at night before going to bed. Our chapel is a very simple space, and I am almost always alone there. As I reflect on it now, I realize that my prayer times normally begin in one of three ways. Most common is to begin by reading the gospel of the day and noticing which phrase or incident catches my attention. Then I ask what God is trying to communicate to me in this word and ponder what it means for my life. My mind may wander, but I come back to the word as if to a lamp placed in the center of the room. Its light sometimes seems dim and flickering, other times startlingly bright; but there is usually an illumination there that marks the rest of the day.

A second way my prayer may begin is by reflecting on something that is disturbing me. This may be a difficulty or issue in my own life, or it may be a local or world event. Sometimes, I must admit, I can get stuck in just worrying about the issue. When I really enter into prayer with it, though, I almost always come to some insight into how different God's perspective on this problem is from those of most of the human players, myself included. Often relevant Scripture passages come to mind and help with this process. I find that I sometimes resist these new perspectives, because they demand a lot of me if I really dare to let them replace my natural reactions. Yet over time I believe this process is how the phrase from our Constitutions about "taking on the feelings and preferences of his Heart" can gradually become a reality in my life.

The third way that my prayer may begin is a more immediate and radical contemplative approach. Often this is how I pray at night, with only a small nightlight on in the chapel. I close my eyes and simply am present to God within. I surrender to the work of the Spirit, who quietly makes something new out of the rags of my life. This intimacy of the Spirit can be agonizing when wounds are touched. Other times it is great joy and full of God's flowing fruitfulness. My favorite Scripture passage for this is "Let all who thirst come to me" (Isaiah 55:1). Sometimes thirst is painful, while at other times it is the joy of the living water flowing from his Heart.

In these most contemplative moments I find a paradox of solitude and community. I am deeply solitary, alone with God, yet more aware than at any other time of how my life and being are formed in a web of relationships. It is a time to embrace others with an openness that forgives all that has been hurtful, rejoices in what is life-giving and prays for the flow of grace in present and future need. In such moments I am most aware of how the deepest truth is that Christ companions us all, bearing our burdens and making them light.

But prayer cannot be only solitary and contemplative. In our community, we usually go to the chapel for fifteen or twenty minutes of communal prayer after dinner. We read the next day's gospel aloud, spend a few minutes in contemplative silence and offer reflections and petitions. To be honest, this is not usually a very deep time for me, as more often than not I am tired and distracted. Yet I know it is important that we put our bodies on the line in this way, affirming to one another and to God that we are women of prayer *together*, not just singly.

The same is true for attending Mass. The logistical scramble of my life means that I often don't make it to daily Mass. But when I do, even though I am frequently less recollected than I should be, the Eucharist is a profound encounter for me. Both the flame of God's self-giving and the flame of my fellow participants' faith move me deeply.

To a young person just awakening to prayer, I would say that it is truly a lifelong journey. Some parts of this journey are more like travel in the days of oxcarts and bare feet than like the high-tech travel of our own times. There will be times of feeling lost and confused, of being overwhelmed by bad weather and bad logistics, of nearly despairing that you will ever get to your destination. There will also be good times, amazing times, when everything truly seems to work together for good! The key words to remember on this journey are trust, surrender, fidelity, mercy. With these, you will always find your way. ∽

A Scaffolding for Prayer

Joan Gannon, RSCJ

Two of the gifts of my almost-elder years are an absolute conviction that God and I are one, and a long morning for prayer. A result of the first is that I know with certainty that every impulse of my heart – even negative ones that are cries for help – is prayer. A result of the second is that I can indulge my need to enjoy that conviction.

The three or so hours I have for formal prayer are disciplined and patterned. The heart of that time is a period of centering prayer,* something I began about forty years ago when I became aware that the Spirit of God within me, as Paul says, knows best how to pray and that she needs only my quiet mantra breathing and the gentle release of any focused thought to accompany her. Before that time I prepare: two journal pages written quickly to the Beloved (from my late teens my name for God) in stream of consciousness, a way of letting go of thoughts that might otherwise demand my attention later, and morning prayer from *Give Us This Day*,* my monthly missalette. Then I sit in a half lotus on my prayer cushion, pray that "you give me your eyes with which to see, your ears with which to hear, your mind with which to judge and to understand, your heart with which to love," and "Draw me into your relationship with the Father and the Holy Spirit," and surrender myself.

I am grateful that not only is every impulse of my heart a prayer, but that it is always a shared grace, that the communion of saints is a reality. Philippine's Holy Thursday journey* throughout the world, spreading Jesus' saving blood everywhere, always appealed to me. My journey, when I have ended my centering prayer time, with the plea that God remember the psalmist's promise: God is "close to the broken-hearted and the crushed in spirit God saves" . . . is to go throughout the world, to upwards of one hundred countries now, bringing God's compassion, courage, love and presence to suffering people everywhere.

A few yoga *asanas** coupled with my own formulaic phrases give my body an opportunity to pray, and then I sit reflectively to read the day's offerings from *Give Us This Day*. If there is still time, I may also read from my current spiritual book for a brief time.

Finally, a walk! In some ways, coming as it does at the end of this time, it winds up being the most focused and intimate time with my Beloved. It is also the time during which I send the energy of love to the natural world, particularly the little lake at the bottom of our hill and bodies of water everywhere, and ask various of my friends and holy ones on the other side to care for family, friends, those to whom I have promised prayer. No one has ever dropped off my list, so it is quite long!

In no sense do I believe God needs any of this from me. I know without a doubt God's transforming love is at work in me and in all the world without my bringing it to God's attention. But I need it. I need to remind myself of all the people to whom I am grateful, all the people for whom and with whom I offer my life. In this blessed gift of time, I am profoundly aware, in the words of e. e. cummings, that at every other moment "I carry your heart with me (I carry it in my heart) . . ." I am aware that we are one. ∽

The Society's call to contemplation,
a compelling love written in our hearts by the Spirit,
makes us seek and cherish
prolonged times of prayer.

—Constitutions of the Society of the Sacred Heart §24

The Importance of Choices

Nancy Ghio, RSCJ

Arriving at my eightieth year proved to be an unusual experience. I had given much thought to our probation devise:* "What can separate us from the love of Christ?" The understanding of these words has gradually opened out to me.

Praying these words through the years, two questions came to mind: will my choice become a barrier between me and God, or will my choice bring me near to God? Using these questions during my eighties has brought peace and happiness to my life.

∽

Speak little, pray much, go onward always, letting passing things pass by, holding only onto what is eternal.

—Saint Madeleine Sophie Barat

All Is Yours Now

Frances M. Gimber, RSCJ

Some weeks ago we were either singing or talking about St. Ignatius' *Suscipe*.* I remembered the line in the St. Louis Jesuits' version: "All is yours now." That particular formulation has stayed with me; it comes to mind at odd moments; it dominates my prayer; it offers a means of turning to God within in every situation, whether happy or not so happy. Of course, we know that it is always true that everything is God's, from the beginning of our lives until the end; prayer for me seems to be the process of growing into that awareness, of coming to believe practically that all is God's.

At the time of my profession* two different people sent me the same holy card with their message of congratulations. The picture was of a chalice and paten with the words, *Être devant Dieu en* état *d'offrande*; to be before God as an offering. The people who chose to send me that card did not know that the name of our probation* was the "spirit of adoration," with a *devise** taken from the *Adoro Te*.* The words of Jesuit Gerard Manley Hopkins' translation are "Low lies here a heart, lost, all lost in wonder at the God thou art." It has often been said in the Society that the name given to one's probation was a program for life. In my case that has proved true. Before the mystery of God what attitude is possible, except adoration? The message came from all sides.

What do I do now? Like everyone formed more than fifty years ago, I was taught Ignatian* meditation but introduced to simple prayer and encouraged to follow my own inclination when the formula of composition of place and three points ceased to seem like prayer. My time in Japan introduced me to Zen and to the concepts of emptiness and formlessness that underlie Zen practice. Though Zen is not my practice now, I find myself more and more following the advice of William Johnston, SJ, a Zen practitioner, who tells us to "sit with the symbol." Sometimes the symbol is a thought, for example, "All is yours now." In spite of all one reads about getting beyond thought, it is my experience that to hold one thought in my consciousness helps to dispel the innumerable other thoughts, memories, images that I want to get rid of at prayer time. At other times, and lately, I sit for half an hour before the Blessed Sacrament and then the thought is simple presence. And that leads back to adoration and being before God as offering.

I have always been deeply interested in language, so the first verse of John's gospel has always spoken to me. "In the beginning was the Word," and the Word remains my image of God, God's way of communication, whether the Word of the Scriptures or words spoken or written by people I come in contact with. That image has become the integrating principle of my prayer life and my work. We were taught in the noviceship* to love Scripture and to continue to read it all our life. From childhood I have loved the liturgy, and that love has survived all the variations recent years have introduced. Its union of word and sacrament I find nourishing, even when unsatisfying aesthetically. For the last several years I have come to reading the Office* almost every day as a means of using the Scripture, especially the psalms, of course. Sometimes I recite the psalms of the Office in the name of suffering people whom I don't know and will never meet, but whose stories are reported at every turn. It is a way of extending my prayer to a world beyond and of keeping me aware of that world beyond my own limited circle. Besides, as Paul says, "We do not know how to pray as we ought." I believe that to pray with the liturgy is a way of overcoming that inability, a way of allowing the Spirit to pray within us.

I am writing at the end of the Easter season when we are reading John on oneness with the Father, with Christ, a profound expression of the Mystery, which I do not understand any better now than I did earlier, but I am filled with gratitude that I have been called to stake my life on it. ⁓

Praying in a Questioning Way

Carol Haggarty, RSCJ

For me there are many ways to pray: centering prayer,* Ignation prayer,* *lectio divina**
to name a few. I am also drawn to prayer in times of sorrow, loss, need. I pray when I
need to express gratitude or joy, or gain insight into a problem or situation. So recognizing the need for prayer, I come to reflect on the question: how do I pray?

The *Constitutions of the Society of the Sacred Heart** contain these illuminating words:

> *We cannot glorify the adorable*
> *Heart of Jesus worthily*
> *except inasmuch as we apply ourselves*
> *to study His interior dispositions*
> *in order to unite and conform ourselves to them.*
>
> *Jesus calls us*
> *to a personal encounter with Him.*
> *He wants to make known to us*
> *the feelings and the preferences of His Heart.*
>
> *In the Gospel*
> *through His words, His attitudes,*
> *His relationships with people,*
> *His way of relating to all created things,*
> *we discover His Heart*
> *wholly given to the Father and to all people.*

(§ 17-19)

With these words in mind, I often pray with the Scriptures, but in a questioning way.
Let me explain with an example. Consider the story of the sinful woman forgiven in
Luke 7: 36-50.

I ask the woman, "Why did you go to Jesus at the home of Simon the Pharisee?" She answers, "I had heard about him and even heard him speak. As I listened to him, I knew that something was awakening in my heart that had been closed and unknown to me. How was I acting and dealing with others and myself? Was I being as loving as he was when he showed us how people could act toward and love one another? The more he talked, the more my defenses cracked, and I could articulate to myself what was hindering me from being loving toward others and myself. He helped me peel away the layers of hardness and control, to look at motives for my actions and much more."

I hear her continuing, "So why did I really go to the home of Simon? It was because I was forgiven, and also because I became more aware of my sins and then could decide what to do about them. I saw a new way of being, so I came to give thanks, to show love openly with the aid of the oil and the anointing of Jesus' feet. I did not need to talk to Jesus; I needed to do something that showed him my gratitude, love and care in a gentle, perhaps intimate, way. It is more common to anoint another's head, but I anointed his feet – I had to do it in a way that had meaning for me and one that I hoped Jesus would understand. I am sure you noticed that it was my tears that first were on his feet, and it was those tears that I wiped away with my hair. As he had cleansed me, so I cleansed him before applying the oil. In that anointing, I believe that I was anointed too."

"Did you hear what Jesus said to Simon about me? He spoke of my many sins, but said that they were forgiven and that because of that I could show great love. Ponder that for a while. Jesus' last words to me were, 'Your faith has saved you; go in peace.'"

I then ask her, "Now that he is gone – how are you doing?" She answered, "Well, in my daily life, I try to remember what it felt like to be near him, to touch him, to listen to him. It is not the same, but my faith has increased. I feel his presence during the day because I try to see with his eyes, understand with his knowledge, and try to act out of his wisdom. Again I tell you that when I anointed his feet it was as if he was anointing me, and that is what I live out of every day."

The next part of my prayer with this woman is to ask Jesus, in her presence, "Jesus, what were you thinking while this woman anointed your feet?" But I leave that answer and dialogue up to you. Once you have had the dialogue with Jesus, think back on it and ask yourself, "Was Jesus talking about the woman who anointed his feet or was he talking about me?"

This is just one way I pray, but it leads me to a personal encounter with Jesus to discover his Heart in order to glorify him. Prayer is essentially what God does, how God addresses us, looks at us. It is not primarily something we are doing for God but what God is doing for us. Remember, prayer is not a technique but a relationship. The essence of prayer is God. Enjoy your time with God. ✎

Seaward

Linda Hayward, RSCJ

On Saturday I walk to the ocean. I notice the traffic on Sunset Cliffs. I observe the planter box in front of a house, a planter with spreading tomatoes and small rows of lettuce and carrots. I see a sign on a porch pointing to pier and shore and Dog Beach. One newly painted house gleams yellow in the sun. Morning glories climb the fence around a vacant lot. A couch, chairs, chests, coolers cram another porch.

On the beach an early bird erects volleyball nets and outlines the courts in rope. I cross the sand to where waves send foam ashore and spread my jacket to sit upon. The vastness of the sea, the rhythm of the waves, the balance of the surfers tell the mighty power of God. The houses on the way attest to God-at-work in people's lives.

I talk with Jesus who called the fishermen, who sat in a boat to preach, who walked on water and calmed the storm, who filled empty nets and served breakfast on the beach. I listen to Jesus who calls me to see, to continue to respond to the call, to love people and life and live it to the full. ～

To go into the presence of God is like going out into the freshness of the morning air. God is always new and his presence gives new life. So the Act of the presence of God acts like a breath of spring air to our soul, calming, refreshing, invigorating.

—Janet Erskine Stuart, RSCJ

Union with God

Ellen Justine Hoffman, RSCJ

Because I cannot see or hear, I can't do anything, so I pray all day. I have many hours in the chapel where I just hold my hands open and offer to God all the people and intentions I've been asked to pray for. I ask Our Lord to do what is best for each person and situation. I just sit before God in my wheelchair and ask God to take care of whatever the problem of the moment is.

In my room, during the day, I say the fifteen decades of the rosary. It unites me to what Jesus and Mary went through in their lives, and it is a way of union with God.

Prayer for me is union with God. It's entrusting myself into God's hands and talking to God. I thank God all the time that we have Mass and communion every day. We are so blessed here at Oakwood.* We are surrounded by love and beauty. ～

Learning from Mary, who pondered all things in her heart, we try to develop awareness and a contemplative outlook that will help us to be thankful for the diversity, depth and beauty of the world and to feel the divine mystery within it.

—Society of the Sacred Heart, *Life Unfolding*, 20.

Counting to Ten

Mary Hotz, RSCJ

How do I pray? I am not sure, exactly. My intention is to sit down, feet flat on the floor, back straight, and begin by focusing on my breath and trying to count to ten without distraction. When some thought tangle presents itself, right before I arrive at two, I breathe deeply, and return to one. It looks something like an odd computer code: 1 . . . 2 . . . 1 . . . 2 . . . 1 . . . 2 . . . 3 . . . 1 . . . .

Once, when I was teaching Laurence Sterne's *Tristram Shandy*, an 18th-century novel about the machinations of the mind, I asked students to quietly count to 10 without distraction. When we finished several minutes of meditation, I asked the class to write down their distractions in order to have them appreciate what Sterne accomplishes in his wacky novel. One student chimed in immediately, "I am still thinking about those red shoes at Macy's." Perfect.

Whether red shoes, lunch, appointments, instant replay of one moment after another, the endeavor to be present to Christ, however frail and unstable, is the prayer. The point, I think, is to make room for the incarnation. ⌒⌒

Be Still and Wait in Patience

Kathleen Hughes, RSCJ

As I begin to write about prayer, I think of a verse of today's psalm, which I read this morning: "Be still before the Lord and wait in patience" (Ps. 37:7). That is an apt description of my prayer at this stage of my life, but it was not always so. My prayer has shifted and changed over many years in tandem with the changing circumstances of my life and the growing depth of my relationship with the God of my life.

I cannot remember a time when I did not pray, though I'm not sure I thought of it that way as a child. I remember my first grade teacher asking me: "Do you love Jesus?" How puzzled I was. Of course! Jesus was simply my best friend. I talked to him on my way home from school and sometimes while falling asleep at night. I shared hurts as well as happiness, doubts, desires, questions, whatever was on my mind, whatever was in my heart.

Once I realized that none of my friends talked to Jesus, he became my secret friend, gradually filling me with a desire to know something more about holiness and the holy life. In high school I learned that some of the saints had spiritual guides, so I asked a Jesuit in my parish to be my director. We parted company when I was given some weird practices like kissing the floor. I didn't want to be that holy! Also in high school I started to go to daily Mass, drawn both by this mysterious ritual that I loved and by a drop-dead handsome boy who sat on the other side of the church.

At Newton College of the Sacred Heart I continued to be drawn to the Eucharist and even more attracted to adoration followed by benediction on Sunday afternoons. The Newton College chapel itself was a mysterious place. It was a low-ceilinged basement room under Barat House, down a long, windowless corridor. It was like a cave, and it lent itself to the intimacy of the rituals celebrated there. Adoration was new and deeply moving for me – candles, flowers, incense and utter stillness all contributed to my absolute conviction of being in the presence of the divine in a wordless exchange. It was adoration and benediction that nurtured in me the desire to give my life to God completely and to throw in my lot with the Religious of the Sacred Heart of Jesus.

Formation in the Society of the Sacred Heart included a rigorous school of prayer – incorporating an amazing assortment of prayer types. Day began with an hour of meditation followed by the chanting of the morning Office* and then Mass. The shorter mid-day hours,* vespers* and compline* completed our celebration of the Office, but the day was also interspersed with two examens* of conscience, spiritual reading in common, the rosary and, to my great delight, a half hour of adoration – a time of utter stillness and union with God in the midst of this boot camp of prayer!

Obviously, not every form of prayer is nourishing for everyone. But as I reflect back, I realize that I was being trained in a variety of patterns that would serve me well as my ministry changed and my prayer life waxed and waned. Through the recitation of the Office I came to love the psalms, and my devotion to them only deepened when a graduate school professor called them "the prayer book of Jesus," and pointed out that they expressed every human heart cry, whether praise or pain or petition. To this day, I usually begin my prayer with the words of a psalm.

Boot camp learnings also included a pattern of meditation on the Scriptures that gradually became my point of departure for simply pondering the word of God and the actions of Jesus. The Ignatian pattern of the examen, a review of the day, has had a patchy place in my prayer repertoire; I believe in its efficacy but forget to make room for it with any regularity. And, after the experience of a pretty chaotic family rosary, I have not since been drawn to the rosary as such, but have learned the value of repetitive prayer, a simple mantra for example, on days when I can only describe my presence before God as "monkey-mind."

After demanding ministries in two Network schools forced me to find time and "heart space" for prayer as best I could, graduate studies in sacramental theology and liturgy transformed my understanding and practice of prayer in ways I would not have imagined. Love of the Eucharist was the reason I was studying in the first place. But I was learning too much and becoming too attentive to the surface performance of the rite and to the performers! I wondered if I would ever be able to pray again at the Eucharist. After a few months, this occupational hazard passed, and I was back to the deeper dimension of Eucharist – joining myself to Jesus' death for the life of the world – though sometimes, even to this day, I still have to close my eyes!

At about the same time, I found my solitary prayer dry and disappointing. Thankfully I had a spiritual director who told me it was harder for a student to pray than almost anyone else. As a student I read all day long, so the use of Scripture for prayer, my mainstay, was no longer nourishing. It was one more thing to read. Happily, I had a fallback. A few years earlier I had learned to play the guitar and had even started to compose songs for the liturgy by setting favorite psalms and pieces of poetry to music. Music gave me a brand new language for prayer. During those heady days, music opened my heart.

I have been blessed to live among women who have valued both solitary and communal prayer. The utter stillness of the early morning hours provides an added incentive to faithful solitary prayer, knowing my sisters are also in communion with God and that this time of prayer is what supports and sustains our active ministries. In fact, it is the fidelity of my sisters that keeps me faithful to daily prayer in the midst of busy stretches or prayer filled with distractions or the dark times of absence, confusion or doubt. Praying together, usually in the evening before dinner, is another discipline that I find personally nourishing. As we take turns planning and leading prayer – sometimes with images or music or silence – we get little glimpses into one another's ways of prayer and insights into the Scriptures, even as our hearts are stretched by one another's deep longings for our world through intercession.

I had, at one time, thought of intercessory prayer as pretty far down on the prayer totem pole. That took a dramatic turn when I was in provincial leadership. Relationships are key to Saint Madeleine Sophie's* form of governance. Day in and day out, I found myself in important conversations with my sisters, and sometimes also with Sacred Heart colleagues, about their lives – prayer, work, community, family, friends – and their hopes and their anguish and struggles. I often concluded a visit asking "What do you want me to pray for?" and I took that promise seriously. Ever since then, my solitary prayer became more and more "peopled," as I entrusted to the Heart of God those for whom I had promised to pray.

In the first Constitutions of the Society (1815) we read: "The spirit of the Society is essentially based upon prayer and the interior life since we cannot glorify the adorable Heart of Jesus worthily except inasmuch as we apply ourselves to study His interior dispositions in order to unite and conform ourselves to them." Those words represent Saint Madeleine Sophie's conviction of the essence of our lives – prayer and the interior life – always the two together. For her there were not discrete times for prayer and then everything else. No, the boundaries of formal prayer are porous, and in the deepest part of our being we try to remain united to Jesus throughout the day, whatever our occupation.

My prayer now? I think I have come to understand what Sophie taught us when she joined prayer and the interior life. Times of prayer don't ever seem like beginning or ending, only becoming more explicitly conscious of an enduring encounter with a precious friend. Over these many years, trying many forms and learning from many companions on the way, prayer has gradually become simpler. It is, after all, rooted in a growing and deepening friendship with God, with Christ, with the Spirit. There are long stretches of companionable silence. In a way, like old friends, words are far less necessary between us. But I know beyond a shadow of a doubt that my heart is being read; the people and situations I bring are being embraced; the events of the day ahead are being blessed. And I know, too, that I am being gradually and imperceptibly transformed in this priceless relationship. It is all grace. ∿

Prayer

It is not that a prayer in anguish
is shorter and more deeply felt
than other prayers.
It is uttered without a single word, a single tear.
It cannot be described
because it is taken into God
before it is even known.
Before the heart is aware
of its need to cry out
it has been heard
in pain just one breadth long.

—Virginia O'Meara, RSCJ

Being in Relationship

Nancy C. Kehoe, RSCJ

After many years in religious life, I do not think so much about how I pray – as that differs – but I think about relationship, my relationship with God/Jesus/the Holy Spirit. Just as in any relationship, there are different ways of being together – sometimes it is important to just BE in the presence of the other, and for me that is what centering prayer* is. At other times, if I am out walking, I might talk to Jesus or the Holy Spirit – sharing a concern, trying to figure out why I am distressed, being grateful for beauty or just being observant and walking.

I think of my annual retreat* not so much as a time when I have to accomplish something, make great changes in myself, or great discoveries about God, but more as a vacation with God, a time to enjoy, to be present without all the distractions of my work life. I love poetry, so reading poetry at breakfast is a way for me to be open to ways God/the Spirit speak to me.

As I have gotten older, I more and more pray to the Holy Spirit for guidance. But it is all about relationship, spending time, being attentive, noticing when I am "not in touch," being grateful and noticing how this relationship has changed me over the years. ∾

The Spirit is always speaking to us deep in our hearts, if only we listen.

—Saint Madeleine Sophie Barat

Going Home

Kimberly M. King, RSCJ

I have prayed in desperation…shaking and keening, and not knowing for certain whether it would ever stop. In those precious moments, all was stripped away and I was left with the most essential – Please. Help. Me.

I have prayed in the midst of throbbing ache and anger…prayed to feel it and to breathe through it…prayed to remain open enough, loose enough, to speak the words Jesus would have me speak and do what needed to be done in the name of Love.

There are times my prayer is simple wonder and gratitude…for the intricacy of a snowflake, the industry of an ant, the way a salad dressing comes together when shaken with a dab of mustard as a binder for the oil and vinegar, the way a word feels in my mouth and the 'inarticulable' diversity of color at day's closing. Sometimes my prayer is simply, "How cool is that? God, you astound me."

I have prayed with friends via Google Hangouts across thousands of miles, prayed in the classroom while witnessing a student's dawning "Aha," and prayed in a fullness of silence both alone and communally. I have shuddered in prayer and intimate concentration while writing essays, poetry and blog entries and while listening to a sonnet, to a choir and to someone across from me. I believe prayer happens with my mouth, my heart, my pen, my disposition and within my being.

On most mornings I pray with coffee, the daily readings and the day's news. In this company and within this context I present myself to God and to the world, desiring to situate myself within the story of my faith and the reality of my world. I do this because for me, it is there, in that overlap of what is most gloriously divine and what is most thoroughly human, that beats the Sacred Heart.

I have known prayer to be a letting go of sorts when I give in to being tired or sad or speechless, or being filled with the AUGH! of beauty or joy; when I realize that there is nothing to say, nothing to do, except be, except open, except offer and receive. At these times, I find grace in ritual when I can let go and let words or gestures wash over me, soothe me, cool my eyes…when I can believe that with just another bit of untethering, I will in fact rise on the music, on the readings, on the palpable nearness of Spirit… and will be home, and am home, after all.

Prayer is my way of drawing back to this home, this center. Prayer is an offering and it is a reminder, a reminder of that essential constant – Nothing can separate you from my love. Nothing. And so I pray… to go on, go through, go forth and to draw in, draw close, to serve, discover and reveal… to open and open and open and, ultimately, to become a part of what I have sought all along and to become a part of what has held me, guided me, strengthened me and nourished me all along.

Returning home time and again has taught me about the stunning beauty and the difficult honor of Love and that Love is my light, my hope and my salvation. ∿

This Stumbling Glory

Mine are the workers, the cities, and fields —
mine is the moonrise, the sunset, the tide.
Eclipses, atoms, tempests, and
flame — mine.
The planets, the fossils, bread broken and shared,
the questions, the journey, this stumbling glory,
mine and all for me. And I am all for them.
And I am all for them —
because I have in me
the expanse of the universe
and in the expanse of the universe —
which includes the perfection of a plum —
is the form, and substance, and beauty of God.

—Kimberly M. King, RSCJ

Meditation Changes One's Life

Joan Kirby, RSCJ

An account of my prayer looks to my best intentions and aspirations so, please understand, I know that is not the whole story. What I say here does not describe the total Joan (though I wish it did). I'm aware of my continuing short fuse, quick retorts that offend and illusions that cloud reality. Still, I will try.

I pray, but I think I really want to share how I meditate. Meditation is different from the ordinary meaning of prayer that can be described as a solemn request for help or expression of gratitude and praise to God. Most people pray, at least those who believe in a higher power; we look outside of ourselves to the all-mighty and all-powerful for help. But as I understand it, in meditation, one is more interior-looking, the mind is calm and silent. Meditation has the possibility of changing one's life.

So, to begin, how do I meditate? When I meditate I go inside myself and observe – try to model my conduct on the dispositions and affections of Jesus – not asking for any special gift or favor, just exposing myself to the influence of my loved one's behavior. I have learned to absorb gospel stories and clearly see compassionate generous loving as a constant in the life of Jesus. The great genius of Saint Madeleine Sophie* was to advise us all to become more like Christ in order to radiate God's love. "I live now, not I, but Christ lives in me" marks the way to identity with Christ. And the Eucharist, where we become what we eat, is the way. In spite of ego interference, I am God's love.

Very young, I was drawn to basking in the light of God's presence. (Most people bask in the sunlight – I do that, too.) But in meditation, I sit quietly and submit to the influence of another. As a novice,* I was gifted with the overwhelming experience of the mystery of God's love, the Father's unspeakable emptying of self to the other, the Son, and the return of love with the same unspeakable dynamism. (Actually, I ate dust to express humility after that exalted experience.)

For years it was enough to sit in silence in the presence of this unimaginably loving God.

It was a wonderful gift, but it did not remain forever. It was tried and tested. And for many years (probably close to sixty) I searched in the darkness for the way to know the

God whom I love… pursuing justice and peace, trying to be poor and caring for the homeless. A period followed when I grew impatient – I was absorbed by too much activity and not enough interior life. I was struggling in darkness, seeking different forms that would bring the gift of God's presence back to life. There were years of distraction, endeavoring to succeed in ministries, growing impatient with words and rituals and practices. At a provincial assembly* I heard a speaker from the Philippines say that the RSCJs in the United States need to cultivate detachment – so much is given to us. It sounded like my love of poverty. I have not forgotten her advice, and it has shaped my future. Little did I know that detachment would mean emptying myself, my ego self, inside and outside – all attachments have to go, words, concepts, self-identity, need for recognition, approval and praise. I am learning what takes the place of my true nature. I wait with open hands that let everything fall out.

In the '90s, I was invited into the interfaith movement where I learned about other traditions and their way to God. In a course I helped design with the dean of Union Theological Seminary, I insisted that we study meditation practices as well as theology, ritual and the sacred writings of seven great traditions. That course opened wonderful riches of spiritual life. Throughout history, many followers of one religious tradition have found their lives transformed and enriched by what they have discovered in another tradition. Hinduism and Buddhism's spiritual practice especially intrigued me. Zen Buddhism, led by a Jesuit priest, seemed "safe" for me to practice. His website quoted his teacher: "I am not trying to make you a Buddhist, but to empty you in imitation of your Lord, Jesus Christ."

Zen Buddhist meditation requires an empty mind. Deep and empty silence appealed, but years of discipline followed in order to silence words, concepts, plans for tomorrow, memories of yesterday, interactions both helpful and sometimes negative – everything that interferes with being awake in the present.

People ask me why I practice Zen Buddhism. I do so because Buddhism has taught me to stop looking for Jesus "out there." For decades I sought to regenerate an inner awareness. I imitated the affections, feelings, attitudes of Jesus, but always as someone, something beyond me – outside – other than me. Buddhism has taught me to stop reaching, looking outside of my inner self…. I am Christ. I receive Christ as my food; I have been permeated by the living Jesus.

So I allow Jesus to live in me, to be me – my True Nature. I look to the Father as Jesus looks, love God as Jesus-the-Christ – no duality…. This is Buddhism's gift to me. Thus what I have learned from Buddhism is that we are not separate – all is one reality. There is no outside/inside. For years I identified with Thich Nhat Hanh's great poem, *Please Call Me by My True Names*, which reads in part:

I am the child in Uganda, all skin and bones,
my legs as thin as bamboo sticks.
And I am the arms merchant,
selling deadly weapons to Uganda.
I am the twelve-year-old girl,
refugee on a small boat,
who throws herself into the ocean
after being raped by a sea pirate.
And I am the pirate,
my heart not yet capable
of seeing and loving.

It is all one reality. So prayer to God "out there" has stopped. We are one with God who is intensely, dynamically, invisibly present. Like Rumi, we swim in the vast ocean of grace, still somehow longing for more.

This prompts me to live in the present moment because this is where God is. The gift here is entrance to another perception of reality where Christ is loving in and through me. It is his gift of self, not mine.

Silent, attentive, alert, loving, yearning in the presence of Mystery characterizes my meditation/prayer these days. I am one of Rumi's *Love Dogs*:

One night a man was crying,
Allah! Allah!
His lips grew sweet with the praising,
until a cynic said,
"So! I have heard you
calling out, but have you ever
gotten any response?"

The man had no answer to that.
He quit praying and fell into a confused sleep.

He dreamed he saw Khidr, the guide of souls,
in a thick, green foliage.
"Why did you stop praising?"
"Because I've never heard anything back."
"This longing you express is the return message."

The grief you cry out from
draws you toward union.

Your pure sadness
that wants help
is the secret cup.

Listen to the moan of a dog for its master.
That whining is the connection.

There are love dogs
no one knows the names of.

Give your life
to be one of them.

—Rumi (1207-1273) ～

Take and Receive

Mary Mardel, RSCJ

To ask how I pray seems like asking how I love. I really don't know how to answer. But I'll try.

I realized during my January retreat that I seldom pray directly to the Father. That surprised me a little, and I have been asking Jesus to lead me to the Father. He is doing that. But mostly my prayer is with Jesus and the Spirit. It gives me great comfort and courage to know that, regardless of how I am feeling, the Spirit is praying in me – all the time, even during the night. So I unite myself to that prayer each night before I go to sleep. During my times of prayer I often unite myself to Jesus' prayer.

In my morning prayer I usually take the gospel of the day for a launching pad – reading it the night before. In the morning I don't do much thinking ... it is more just "being with" – and trying to stay there. Some days it is mostly "Jesus, help me!" and "I love you," repeated many times.

I pray the morning and evening prayers of the Church every day and relish the psalms and many of the antiphons. Something like: "As morning breaks, I look to you, my God, to be my strength this day," can become a refrain all during the day.

"Take and receive" is very much part of my prayer, and I try to honestly mean my favorite prayer, Charles de Foucauld's *Prayer of Abandonment*:

> *Father,*
> *I abandon myself into your hands;*
> *Do with me what you will.*
> *Whatever you may do, I thank you:*
> *I am ready for all, I accept all.*
> *Let only your will be done in me,*
> *and in all creatures.*
> *I wish no more than this, O Lord.*

Into your hands I commend my soul:
I offer it to you with all the love in my heart,
for I love you, Lord, and so need to give myself,
to surrender myself into your hands without reserve,
and with boundless confidence,
for you are my Father.

To me these words express what Jesus' prayer to his Father must have been, and I often ask him to say it with me. It's not so scary that way.

What do I want from prayer? I think it is the grace that I have been praying for ever since my profession: To make each moment of my life a loving, "Yes, Jesus," to all he asks and sends. When I can do that, it takes care of everything.

Contemplating Jesus, we learn
from his attitudes and responses
how, in all our relationships,
to witness to the liberating power of His love.

—Constitutions of the Society of the Sacred Heart §15

Gratitude Pervades

Kathleen McGrath, RSCJ

Before I entered religious life, I negotiated contracts for thirteen years. Terms were agreed upon ahead of time, numbers added up. In my late twenties, when I began to take my relationship with God more seriously, I approached God in the same way. I asked God to lay out the terms of what God wanted me to do, and if agreeable I would consent and follow. God's response in prayer was more like, "trust in me and trust me with all of the details and all will be well." My response was, "I would have to spend more time with you then and get to know you more if I am going to do THAT!"

Thus began real prayer. It was more of "wasting time with God," as they say. My formal prayer time, then, is more about showing up for the time I set aside for this relationship. Sometimes nothing happens (so I have often thought anyway) and sometimes there has just been an outpouring of palpable love and grace. The details of how I will spend time in prayer, I largely leave up to God these days.

Having said that, I must add that there have been many, many opportunities over the years to learn different ways of praying that I have found helpful. Early on, I realized that the way I learned to pray as a child needed to be expanded. Years before entering religious life, I learned many different ways of praying, mainly in lay formation programs. Centering prayer* was the first daily prayer to which I committed myself as an adult. It had an emptying quality to it that felt like preparing earth for seed. This practice has waxed and waned in my life over the years, and recently I have returned to it with more seriousness. It has also begun, in a new way, to converge with the everyday. The muscle, strengthened over the years by the continual letting go and returning to the One I long for, has begun to activate in the midst of ordinary daily distractions. Centering will quite literally be the thing that gets me out of bed in the morning, and that which gets me through difficulties in my day.

I light a candle under some fragrant oil before my formal prayer time in the morning as a way of beginning intentionally. An icon of *Christ Pantocrator** is central in my prayer space. After centering, I often allow some quieting music to help me settle. I like to pray near a window – gazing at the sunrise or flowers. I might spend time just listening or watching birds or the wind rustling leaves, or just feeling God's presence.

The readings of the day are always part of my prayer. These have been an anchor every morning for some decades. At times, I am called deeper into one of the passages – perhaps spending many months with it, allowing it to seep down deep. This is not as often as it once was. Other times, it is reading the mystics in this way – mulling over their words and allowing them to unfold over months. I always have Sophie's* letters somewhere in my prayer space, and it seems as if at just the right time something she wrote to one of her sisters will be the words I need. Often it is listening to *Rezandovoy* on my iPod that opens up the words of Scripture for the day in a tender, gentle way.

Once in a while, capturing something that happens in prayer in a journal is an important part of my prayer. This is especially true if I am discerning something. Later I can look back to see the whole of what God has been doing over a period of time.

The most important part of prayer these days is simply to allow God to lead. Often God leads me into just a very quiet place without much in the way of words.

Extinguishing the candle marks the end of my formal prayer time in the morning. The day, of course, has its own contemplative moments. There are those times when I really see goodness in others – unveiled in a way – when I am overwhelmed by beauty and opened up to an aspect of God, inaccessible to me, through another's prayer. Or, it may simply be God's invitation that comes in life circumstances to be more patient, surrendered and kind.

These experiences may be captured by the examen* at the end of the day. Again, a favorite spot to pray this prayer is near the window, underneath the night sky. The expanse I contemplate there gently draws me into a simple, spontaneous look at the day from God's perspective. It's never how I would have told the story of the day myself. What comes is other than that. Often, what happened in my morning prayer returns – solidifying somehow the grace received. Then a particular person, situation, joy or sorrow, comes into view very clearly. Gratitude pervades. The day has, indeed, been very full of all that has been given, completely undeserved. ∼

What I Cannot Do Without

Jane McKinlay, RSCJ

As I write this I am looking at a sentence on a sheet of paper from 1958, fastened into my journal. I had just shown Reverend Mother Sabine de Valon (superior general, 1958-1967) the vision I hoped to live by for the rest of my life. She wrote, *"Pour en faire une réalité, travailler sérieusement à être une âme de prière."* (To make this a reality, work seriously to be a soul of prayer.)

Mass about five times a week and prayer with community are part of my life. This is because I believe the words, "Blessed are those who are invited to the banquet of the Lord," and because I think prayer together nurtures community. But Mass and community prayer are not what I cannot do without. What I cannot do without is time in the armchair in my room before the activity of the day and before dinner. For a little more than twenty minutes – morning and evening – I move into the embrace of the One who loves me.

I begin by consulting with myself: Right now, how do I want to open myself to God's action? The answer usually comes easily; it suggests a phrase to repeat as I breathe in and out.... I spend the prayer time giving my attention to the phrase, returning to it each time other thoughts come. When the timer softly beeps I notice what is with me. On occasion it is disappointment, as I say to God, "How distracted I am today!" Usually a phrase is with me – the one I began with or a different one. I write it down. It lightens my step. During the day, coming and going, I return to it. Before going to bed, when I look back on the day, I remember it again and see how much it has or has not taken hold.

The phrase I bring to the prayer time varies from day to day and week to week, but – as I look at phrases I use – it seems to me that they all have to do with a longing for relationship with the living God and a longing to be clay in the hands of the Master Potter.

Often I want to rest in God's embrace, and I say, "I'm resting here." I notice my shoulders dropping and air entering my body and quiet pervading the room. At intervals, actually resting, I no longer need to say the phrase.

When I'm fresh from something that is hard to deal with, I include an explanation like, "I rest here, not because painful things don't happen, but because you know what you are doing and it's all love."

The phrase may be "Yes" or some variation of it. Once recently, what I wanted to be with in prayer was "This is *so* okay," "this" being what meets me in the moment. As the day went on and I repeated it from time to time, something happened that annoyed me. So when I said "This is *so* okay," it was hollow. I was annoyed, not okay. Then I saw that an incident was taking from me something I am attached to. I felt ashamed and humiliated. Finally, I remembered Sophie's* love of humility. I was humbled. And that is *so* okay!

I have very poor hearing. It's painful in many ways. One is with good sitcoms, where getting a clever line delights me. Sometimes, when someone tells me the riposte, I feel sorry for myself because of the many smart lines I know I'm missing. When my sense of loss hangs on, as I approach prayer I want to say, "Yes," and here the yes means acceptance of what I miss because of my poor hearing.

The other day, petty, selfish, judgmental feelings occupied my inner space, and I went to bed that way. I dreamt that I and others were being offered shoots of plants that we could tend and grow. One was quite large, already partly developed. But I chose a small ugly clump – a bit of misshapen green attached to a little dirt. I would water it and tend it. I woke up with this dream in my head, and for prayer I said, "Change this ugly plant."

After a self-indulgent day that left a bad taste in my mouth and a sense of how limited my sights are, the phrase that came to me was, "Stretch me."

Sometimes painful memories from decades past attack me. As I sink into God's embrace, what is clear is, "That was then; this is now."

I am often aware that at every moment I get to choose what I give my attention to. I want to say, "This moment I can choose what is life-giving." By the end of the prayer time it may evolve into "This grand opportunity."

Other times, not wanting to miss the gift of the moment – being loved by the living God – I say, "I'm here, now, for this." Sometimes, it is "I let you love me."

I see God as fashioning something impossible to describe, millennium by millennium, and I want my life to be at the service of that, whatever it is. At times, the phrase that comes is, "I'm available."

What I do in the armchair comes from a longing for intimacy with God – the Trinity – and a longing to be permeated, infiltrated, taken over by, malleable to the living God's creative, healing, sanctifying, ever-fresh action. Words from Psalm 42, "As a deer longs for running streams," express my yearning for both the closeness and the effect of imbibing the transforming water.

My heart seeks the One whom I love, and for about thirty-five years I've been moving around in – sometimes experimenting unsuccessfully with – variations of the way to pray I have described. I am reassured by Sophie: "It doesn't matter how you pray, as long as your heart seeks the One whom you love." ∿

The Mystery of Prayer: The Power of Love

Margaret Mary Miller, RSCJ

When I think about prayer, I wonder if it is really I who pray. Rather, I think it is the Holy Spirit, Jesus, and the Father. Prayer is the Trinity praying in me. I am reminded of the experience of Janet Erskine Stuart, RSCJ.* As she was searching for who she wanted to be and what she wanted to do with her life, she was walking to a chapel to pray. She, a convert to Catholicism, was thinking of her next step in life. A lover of nature, she saw some beautiful hyacinths. All of a sudden she heard inside her heart and her whole being a word from God. As she said later, "then and there, standing by a bed of blue hyacinths, *factum est ad me verbum Dei*, (the word of God came to me) and I saw it all."

When I pray, I like to listen to Jesus. Did not his Father say: "Listen to him" at the transfiguration and at his baptism? His mother, as well, at the Wedding Feast of Cana, said "Do whatever He tells you." I recently read a reflection entitled "Listen to the Deepening Places," the equivalent of "Listen to Him." Listening in prayer to the deepening places is what I like to do.

I like to pray this way because I find that Jesus takes me all over the world. I can pray with him, the Holy Spirit and the Father any place in the world and for all occasions: for the needy, for those suffering in various ways, for the many intentions confided to me, for those hospitalized, for countries lacking peace and justice. I am never wanting in this form of prayer, which I experience as a true gift.

Of course, I pray in other ways as well. I like to use my imagination. For example, I walk back with Mary from the burial of her husband, Joseph, and I learn so much more about Joseph through her eyes and heart. I have also walked with Mary back to her little house after the burial of Jesus. I can see the faces of so many people on her face; her love of each one was like that of her Son who died for each one of us.

If I have a problem, I take a passage from Scripture and pray with it. Let me give you an example. Once, after completing some years of a ministry, I wondered where I could serve next. I thought a lot and decided to get a degree in music, one that I could use to assist people for many years. I had applied, had my audition, was accepted and had everything in place. Then I went to one of our general chapters* and there I was asked to go to Uganda. I thought about it, but it was a dilemma for me. I turned to the story of the Samaritan woman, prayed with it and could feel and hear Jesus say to me: If you knew the gift of living water, perhaps you would ask and He would give you living water. I felt "This is it. This is what I want: living water." I chose to go to Uganda and was at perfect peace. I was able to teach and give workshops and I loved every minute there.

The Eucharist is a top priority in my prayer. This has been true since my childhood. I also love the Liturgy of the Hours* and try to pray with others throughout the world – praying for and with the church and for the world in general, particularly for world peace and justice.

I pray the rosary while walking around a sports track. I give this time to pray, by name, for all of the persons whom I know who have died.

Indeed, there are many other forms of prayer in my life. The above-mentioned give an overview of my ways of prayer. Mostly, I realize that prayer is a Mystery and it is a power of Love. And what a gift that is. I am deeply grateful and exceedingly humbled that God is in me and with me, leading and guiding me in each moment of each day. I am exceedingly grateful, too, that I can lean upon Scripture, which calls me and leads me to be "formed by the Word," a favorite way to pray and to live that I learned from Walter Burghardt, SJ, who always spoke of being formed by the word and the Word . . . one more way of saying that it is Jesus and the Spirit who pray in me. 〜

*The spirit is always speaking to us deep in our hearts,
if only we listen.*

—Saint Madeleine Sophie Barat

You Gave Me Wonder

Shirley Miller, RSCJ

*Prayer is our humble answer to the inconceivable surprise of
living. It is all we can offer in return for the mystery by which
we live . . . only one response can maintain us: gratefulness
for witnessing the wonder, for the gift of our unearned right
to serve, to adore and to fulfill.*

—Abraham Heschel

Photography has been a way of praying for me, "of witnessing the wonder," most of my life. When I was a child, I used to borrow Dad's Brownie camera and wander around the woods, listen for the birds, take photos of them or watch a lone leaf hanging from a branch or a flower growing out of broken cement. I was intrigued by what I could see through a lens. It was a contemplative calling to me long before I understood what that meant. A simple solitary walk in the woods became a life-long pilgrimage.

"In everyone's life there are moments when there is a lifting of the veil at the horizon of the known, opening a sight of the eternal" (Heschel). The camera provides that opening for me, the lifting of the veil, the long view, the close up, the panorama. It helps me focus, stop, gaze and be wrapped in wonder, awe and gratitude. I hear better with a camera in hand. It calls me beyond where I am or more deeply into the moment. In Mary Oliver's words, "Walk slowly; bow often." It helps me see with the eyes of the heart, to enter more fully into the grace-filled-ness of creation, and to encounter the sacred everywhere.

Photography is a healing prayer for me. At times of discouragement, weariness or confusion, when I walk the beach or wander in a garden or on a mountainside or stop by the side of the road to watch the wind in the wheat fields or the light breaking through an abandoned farm house, I find deep peace – not just for that moment but whenever I look at the photo. I remember what I saw, what I felt, what I knew to be true.

The sacredness of creation overflows everywhere: the barren tree against the winter sky, the morning dew on the dandelion, the red cardinal resting on the snow, the eagle soaring high above the trees, the morning star in the black sky, the great blue heron standing erect at sea's edge, or the dolphins dancing in the distance. "Bow often."

The camera draws me into Scripture: finding sunglasses covered with barnacles, washed up on the shore, "Do not forget the things your eyes have seen nor let them slip from your heart all the days of your lives" (Deuteronomy 4:9). It is an invitation to remember what my eyes have seen, to be grateful that I have eyes to see and a heart to remember. It is an opportunity to pray for the person who lost the glasses and to reflect on what she might have seen. I remember....

Two deer walking toward one another, crossing a stream and kissing in mid-stream in the light of a golden autumn afternoon. "Love and faithfulness shall meet; justice and peace shall kiss" (Psalm 85:10). I ask for the grace to reach out to others, beyond myself, across whatever chasms divide me from others. I remember....

A perfect shell I found on the shore. When I picked it up, the hermit crab crawled out and began its dangerous walk back to the sea. He left the shell just for me. I knew more deeply at that moment the meaning of incarnation. "He emptied himself" (Philippians 2:7). I remember....

An extraordinary dawn – darkness and dawn, side by side – the crimson dawn slowly overtaking the dark sky, until the whole world was aflame, and the darkness disappeared. "The light shines in the darkness, a light that darkness could not overpower" (John 1:5). I remember....

Finding a child's abandoned red bucket, lying in the sand on its side at sunset. I felt one with that bucket. I, too, felt alone and empty and tired. I carried the image as I walked the beach. When I returned from my walk the red bucket had been transformed into golden sunlight, and I, too, felt transformed, renewed and I had a glimpse of what resurrection will be like. "Then I saw a new heaven and a new earth . . . I am making all things new" (Revelation 21:1, 5). I remember . . . .

A petrified tree on the shore along the seventeen-mile drive near Carmel. I stopped the car because it was such an extraordinary image of the crucified Christ. As I sat by the tree, a beautiful light began to stream from the face of Christ. "We with our unveiled faces reflecting like mirrors the brightness of the Lord, all grow brighter and brighter as we are turned into the image that we reflect" (2 Corinthians 3:17-18). I remember . . . .

The camera helps me understand the connectedness of all creation and my part in it. Every action of mine somehow mysteriously affects the entire universe; the heart of that universe, in Pierre Teilhard de Chardin's words, is the Heart of Christ. Jesus' desire that all may be one, and Sophie's* desire that we be one heart and one soul in the Heart of Jesus, are invitations to praise God for the wonders of the earth, for the love that binds us together and makes us one, and "to guard that something precious which has been given to us with the help of the Holy Spirit who lives among us" (2 Timothy 1:14).

Photography is a way for me to experience God's immaculate conception of the world – all is holy, all is sacred, all is light shining from the face of Christ. My only response can be "gratefulness for witnessing the wonder, for the gift of our unearned right to serve, to adore, to fulfill." I remember, and I believe.

Prayer: "Something Understood . . . "

Marcia O'Dea, RSCJ

> *Prayer the church's banquet, angel's age,*
>   *God's breath in man returning to his birth,*
>   *The soul in paraphrase, heart in pilgrimage,*
> *The Christian plummet sounding heav'n and earth*
> *Engine against th' Almighty, sinner's tow'r,*
>   *Reversed thunder, Christ-side-piercing spear,*
>   *The six-days world transposing in an hour,*
> *A kind of tune, which all things hear and fear;*
> *Softness, and peace, and joy, and love, and bliss,*
>   *Exalted manna, gladness of the best,*
>   *Heaven in ordinary, man well drest,*
> *The milky way, the bird of Paradise,*
>   *Church-bells beyond the stars heard, the soul's blood,*
>   *The land of spices; something understood.*

—George Herbert (1593-1633)

Saint Madeleine Sophie* in her *Constitutions and Rules of the Society of the Sacred Heart of Jesus* (1815) wrote, "The spirit of the Society is essentially based upon prayer and the interior life." I believe an interior life is the wellspring of joy and understanding in life. But what did Sophie mean by an "interior life"?

First, I believe that this interior spirit is directly related to prayer; it is not simply a time of reflection. While times of reflection and review are needed in our too-efficient lives, a time for prayer is even more important. The British poet, George Herbert, said so well that prayer is "reversed thunder" – that is, it starts with our small sighs but becomes something "clamorous" before the throne of God. He also said that prayer is "something understood"; prayer leads us "to perceive the intended meaning of things," not simply to know them. As a time of prayer ends, I grasp more fully what the questions, communications and relationships in my life mean or imply.

Besides taking me to a place of understanding through prayer, this taking of prolonged time for prayer brings me two other gifts: a spirit of contemplation and the quality of sincerity. Saint Madeleine Sophie said that contemplation is a compelling love written in our hearts by the Holy Spirit. It is a way of stepping back from relationships or challenges and bringing love to them. Rather than gripping tightly onto what life gives me, be it a person, event or decision, I, through contemplation, am able to relax my hold on things so that love and self-giving can seep into my perspective. A contemplative spirit flowing from prayer frees me to love God and serve others better.

Gerard Manley Hopkins, SJ, the Irish poet, says well how prayer leads one to be sincere. In his poem "As Kingfishers Catch Fire," he wrote,

> [He writes of hanging bells]. . . each hung bell's
> Bow swung finds tongue to fling out broad its name;
> Each mortal thing does one thing and the same:
> Deals out that being indoors each one dwells;
> Selves – goes itself; myself it speaks and spells,
> Crying What I do is me: for that I came.

I convey to others what prayer leads me to understand, believe in and cherish; to "speak and spell" myself well in what I do, I must lean on my God and a contemplative view of life. To give others less than what is in my "heart in pilgrimage" is to deny them a very particular gift from me; I may deny another something precious, such as a word or deed of affection, of thankfulness or of encouragement because I listened less openly to the Holy Spirit.

Prayer not only has immense power before God; it builds this interior life, which cannot help but bestow on us some "softness, and peace, and joy, and love" – to quote Herbert – in our relationships with others. As Maya Angelou wrote: "Listen to yourself and in your quietude you may hear the voice of God."

For me, prayer means that I, in that quietude, come to know the dispositions and preferences of Our Lord, of Christ. It also means that my heart is rooted in an interior place before Our Lord where I discover that something is "understood" and know the compelling love of the Holy Spirit.

Prayer is, again to quote Herbert, "exalted manna"; it is a wonderful bread for us mortals who desire to be "interior persons" as we make our sacred journey through life.
〜

Nourishing the Trinity Within

Uchenna Oluoha, NSCJ*

Prayer is the practice of the presence of God. It is the place where my pride is abandoned, hope is lifted and requests are made. Prayer is the process of admitting my need and dependence upon God. It is the privilege of touching the heart of the Father through the Son of God, Jesus my Lord.

Sometimes I come to the Lord with a fervent request for conversion, healing and other needs, and yet the answers I hope for often do not come. I wonder and often doubt. Yet, I persevere and still trust God. I pray because I know that God hears me, and because I desire to see results. With faith and trust in God, I am consistent in my wait in God's presence. I remember always to abide in these three elements of our Christian calling – faith, hope and charity. Faith is my attitude toward God. Charity is my attitude toward others. Hope is my confidence in myself to succeed.

I feel that prayer changes the one praying because, in prayer, I place before God my complete self in confession and dependence. In Luke 18:13, the tax collector prayed, "God, be merciful to me, a sinner!" There is nothing to hide. In silent supplication, I reach into the deepest part of myself, admitting my needs and failures. In so doing, my heart is quieted, pride is removed, and I enjoy God. I know God is close to me because of the immense peace and joy that fills my life.

How do I pray? My individual prayer at various times of the day consists of psalms, Mass, rosary and silent meditation using a mantra – a word or phrase repeated over and over during meditation – and spiritual reading.

Praying the psalms
The psalms help me to learn to pray with Jesus and like Jesus. They help me to become a person after God's own heart in the midst of my daily activities. Psalms teach me to hide nothing from God, but to bring all that is real into the only relationship that can bless the best and heal the worst in me. No matter what l am feeling – distress, trust, anger or delight – I find the words of the psalms accompany me into God's presence. These prayers give me words to glorify, hope, confess and ask for my needs and those of the whole world.

Silent Prayer

"For God alone my soul waits in silence" (Psalm 62:1). "Be still and know that 1 am God (Ps 46:10). I start my silent prayer by becoming present to God's presence. Seated in a relaxed way, I repeat the name "Jesus" interiorly in tune with my own breathing. I often get distracted with my mind wandering off every now and then, but by gently bringing myself back to my mantra word, I am able to continue the process for about thirty minutes. When I am finished, I conclude with "Glory be to the Father, and to the Son and to the Holy Spirit." What is helpful during this time is a quiet space and a cool temperature. I close my eyes to the outer environment and open my interior being to the One whose presence I share.

Spiritual Reading

I often use some of the Society's spiritual books on Saint Madeleine Sophie Barat* and Saint Rose Philippine Duchesne,* and I use the liturgical readings of the day.

Daily Eucharist and rosary

I believe in attending Mass and receiving the Eucharist daily. It is the sacrifice of all sacrifices because it is the sacrifice of God for me. Like the Blessed Virgin Mary, we become living tabernacles of God after communion. For me, the mystery of the Eucharist is the most perfect form of prayer.

As a teenager growing up in Nigeria, I participated in the life of the parish church by belonging to the Legion of Mary, a lay Catholic association whose members have devotion to the rosary. Every legionary is required to carry out a weekly apostolic work in the spirit of faith and in union with Mary. It is through this practice that I live the balance of contemplation and ministry.

The above forms of prayer energize me and give me a great sense of fulfillment. Since I was accepted into the Society of the Sacred Heart as a candidate,* my prayer life has not changed much, but it is evolving rapidly and getting better. What do I mean by that? I am getting to understand in depth some of the theological reasons behind some of these various ways that I and others pray. In my community, each of the sisters has a unique way of personal prayer. Yet, in the morning, there is great silence in the house with everyone sharing the space in communion with the Divine. It is an experience of wonder and awe.

Recently, I completed a course on "Introduction to the New Testament" at Trinity University, Washington. This course enabled me to appreciate praying with the New Testament passages, especially the gospels and the letters ascribed to Saint Paul. The book of Revelation was scary to pray with before. Since the completion of the course, 1 can now make sense of this book and can understand it better when it appears in my spiritual reading.

Clearly, there are diverse ways of praying. No one way fits all and no form of prayer is excluded. The most important element in all these forms is the act of praying, when we communicate with God. However one chooses to pray depends on personal preference. Prayer is a basic necessity of life, just like food, shelter, water. Without these elements, our body cannot survive. So also, without prayer, our interior life cannot survive. We all need to sustain and nourish the Trinity in us. And how do we begin? We begin by praying. 〜

Contemplation

Virginia O'Meara, RSCJ

I have come
From ancient caves
And caverns
Where I discovered fire.

I came out to light
And air and speech
And thought
To share my gift
By writing sparks
In words which then
Would burn
In a creative blaze
Like the bush
Which Moses saw
And said how it
Would be a sacred sign.

I find instead
That it has taken
All my care
To merely keep
A small and silent
Flame alive
For seeing in the night.

Over the Years

Lyn Osiek, RSCJ

How do I talk about silence? How do I find words to describe no-words? There was a time – many years ago – when I tried the Ignatian* way of pre-designated "points" for meditation, leading to rational considerations, leading to heartwarming affects and purposeful resolutions. This was the gold standard method when I was a novice,* though it was always made clear that we didn't have to follow it. One can even see the influence of this kind of prayer on Philippine* after her initiation into the Society of the Sacred Heart in 1804 led by would-be Jesuits. In Grenoble in January 1806, she meditated on the detachment of the Magi in leaving their own country and applied it to her own desire to imitate them, hindered by her attachment to Sainte Marie.* She knew that if she followed her vocation to foreign lands as the Magi did, she could not also have Sainte Marie. Or later in 1834, when Ignatian methods* of prayer were again imposed on the Society, she said by this time that she couldn't meditate, but just took things whole as she saw them.

I was unable to keep any kind of order in this step-by-step process, and when I tried to meditate on a gospel scene by placing myself in it, I spent all the time trying to make decisions about clothes, hairstyles, etc. Once I began biblical studies, it was really hopeless because I knew too much about what biblical scenes probably looked like and how much they didn't look like the pictures or our contemporary imagination. I couldn't let go of all that to slip into some hazy perception of a story.

Just as I was beginning biblical study, I found a God I could deal with in Zen and yoga, which were both popular at the time. There I found God as mystery, ever inviting deeper commitment in the reality of my life. It wasn't about my going somewhere else but about finding ways to bring God into the here and now.

I used to be asked sometimes about the effects of theological study on my faith. Some are afraid that study will destroy faith. I can only say that the moment when the question came to me: "What if none of this is true?" was the beginning of an exciting journey of deconstruction and building anew that I would not have wanted to miss for anything. I recommend it!

The gospel passages, the Zen, the yoga, have long ago given way to something much simpler. The Greeks were savvy about loving. They had three different words for love – not that they seem always to have been totally clear about the differences. There is *philia:* delight in the other, the love of friendship and sharing of good, the kind of relationship that the Bible says we should have with wisdom (Wisdom 8:18). There is another kind of loving, *erōs,* the love of an object or person that drives us to desire to possess and have the closest possible union with the object of our desire. Desire for God is a foundation of the life of prayer. This is a love that gets us up in the morning and keeps us going. The third kind of love, *agape,* is not so flamboyant. It is the undramatic yet deliberate decision to be for the other. Here is the love from which the author of the Song of Songs speaks in one of the Society's favorite passages, applied to Sophie: "Set me as a seal on your heart, as a seal on your arm, for love is strong as death; many waters cannot quench love" (Song of Songs 8:6-7). I know that real love is not measured or weighed or susceptible to analysis. I also know that my relationship with God includes all three.

Previously, I never followed any kind of daily meditation guide. Lately, since the province* has made *Give Us This Day** available to all of us, I usually turn to it to see what's happening there for the day. But it is not the gospel or the first reading or the saint of the day or the reflection that catches me up. It is the opening line of the psalm for morning prayer. One or two lines of the author's thirsting for God is enough. ∼

All Is Gift!

Clare Pratt, RSCJ

As I approached my seventy-fifth birthday, aware that I was entering the final quarter of my life, I was conscious of the tremendous changes I have seen and lived from the age of four — when, much to my Protestant mother's embarrassment, I insisted on making the sign of the cross and genuflecting on the sidewalk as we passed the local Catholic church — until today.

What has not changed in all these years is my thirst for God — from age thirteen, when I was first aware of my vocation to religious life, to my resolution at the end of my thirty-day retreat* prior to making my final vows in Rome to give prayer the primary place in my life, to the daily ritual of movement to the song from *Missa Gaia* that has begun my prayer for many years: "All of creation resounds with song; bless ye the Lord, praise him forever. Stars in the heavens, waters below, bless ye the Lord, praise Him forever...."

Over the years, I have experienced a growing integration of two gospel mandates: "Pray always and without ceasing" (1 Thessalonians 5:17), and "When you pray, go into your room, shut the door and pray to your Father" (Matthew. 6:6).

In my current ministry as community life director at Oakwood* I have the gift of beginning and ending my day in my bedroom, located in a small apartment, that I share with a variety of RSCJs and guests, three minutes from the Oakwood building. From early evening until 8:25 a.m., it is my hermitage, my sanctuary, a place of silence, where I can rest, read, pray and re-fuel for the coming day.

In the silence that stills my being, I focus on the precious objects in my prayer corner: a crucifix, a candle, Sophie* cradling the infant Jesus, photos of each of my parents holding me as a baby, memorial cards of our recently deceased — evoking the communion of saints and the conviction that they are with us — photos of dear friends, and scenes of waterfalls, mountains and woods. I breathe deeply and let come what comes —

"Be still and know that I am God . . . "

"Take. Lord, receive all my liberty, my memory, understanding, my entire will . . . "

*"Do in me, through me, with me,
without me whatever you will . . . "*

As I leave the apartment and head for our 8:30 a.m. "stand-up" meeting of department heads, "pray always" takes over. Recently it occurred to me that a very relevant image for the way the Holy Spirit accompanies me throughout the day is the image of a GPS: to allow the Spirit to be my GPS. Actually, I do not have a GPS. Though I do look up directions on the internet, I sometimes still use paper maps, a remnant of my childhood when we set off for family vacations with my father at the wheel and I in the passenger seat, the "navigator," with the map spread out on my lap. But I have had many experiences recently that evoke the image of responding to the Spirit "on the spot." It is as if the Spirit is literally directing me down the hall. "Turn left . . . turn right . . . recalculate . . . stop at Sister X's door . . ." helping me to meet Jesus in the face of each one of my sisters, especially those who are most frail and vulnerable, in the faces of our staff, the students of our school, family and friends of our sisters, whomever comes through Oakwood's front door.

For many years I have found God in images: sailboats, butterflies, majestic trees, streams of water, baby swans nestled on their mother's back, airplanes – whose taking off or landing or flying high up in the sky always evoke a line from Christopher Frye's *Sleep of Prisoners:* "The enterprise is exploration into God." In fact, those accompanying me in my annual retreats* through the years have sometimes been amazed at the plethora of images that fill my prayer. But, more recently, thanks to an article from the *Journal of Biblical Literature* on "The Gospel of John and the Five Senses" by Dorothy Lee, an Australian biblical professor at the University of Melbourne Divinity School, I have become more and more conscious of how body and spirit are one – how all of our senses, not only our eyes, are a pathway to union with God.

I love to listen to the song of birds as I walk the paths around our property or the labyrinth in the school courtyard, and I sing Taizé and other refrains. One refrain I love was taught to the delegates of our 2008 General Chapter* in Peru by Sister Gerardette Philips, an Indian RSCJ, who has been living in Indonesia for many years:

*Breathing in, breathing out, I am calm, I am smiling,
You in me, I in You, present moment, wondrous moment,
peace to the world . . . peace to the world.*

I often sing it to myself during the minute of silent prayer for peace we have at Oakwood each day at 12:15 during our mid-day meal.

Which brings me to the sense of taste. Writing these words I am aware of the taste of tears, and over the last months tears have flowed copiously during my morning prayer. As I write this, more than forty countries are experiencing conflict and violence – many over religion! Our own Sister Philomene Tiernan was winging her way back from Europe to her native Australia when the Malaysian airliner on which she was traveling was shot down over Ukraine. More and more I touch the pierced Heart of Jesus in the pierced heart of humanity, aware that what touches someone in a far-off land touches me, touches us.

Finally, what I see and hear, breathe, taste and touch are gathered up in gratitude. Every morning just before leaving the apartment I read the night shift nursing report on e-mail and then open a Word for the Day from gratefulness.org, a website created and managed by followers of Brother David Stendl-Rast, OSB. Quotations are from a variety of sources: the Dalai Lama, Saint Paul, Maya Angelou, Etty Hillesum, Jesus.... I take a moment to savor the words and sometimes pass them on. I desire to grow in an attitude of gratitude, a perfect preparation for the Eucharist I will celebrate in a few minutes.

All is gift: meeting God in my little sanctuary as well as in the smile of a sister whose dementia keeps her in the now. All is gift.... All is gift! ～

Who do you say that I am?

Rose Marie Quilter, RSCJ

Jesus, I say that you are the Anointed One who washes our feet and anoints us to continue your touch. I say that you are the Beloved of God who loves me and teaches me to love through the faces, voices and touch of those who have loved me – and through those who challenge me to grow.

I see your face in my friend who drives me around his city to so many places where those he serves struggle for health, for life, for dignity, for bread. His passion is to be with them to serve them, empowering them in your name.

I see your face in Nellie, who listened to homebound people for thirty years and died seeing her husband, her mother and a roomful of angels and people. Year after year, she "spoke to the weary a word that would rouse them" (Isaiah). Why would they not greet her as she crossed that final river?

I see you in Julie, who was afraid to have her fifth child in ten years, but who sees that child especially as God's gift.

I see you in Jay, in her care for all God's creatures and in her generosity.

I see you in Danny, shot at age nine by a thirteen year old playing with a gun.

I see you in old nuns who love you to their dying breath – especially I see you in Anita, who kept repeating: "Jesus, I desire only you" and who gave her last years to the Haitian poor.

I see you in the humor of my sister Anne, who, after drastic surgery, invited a roomful of anxious friends to "a viewing."

I touch you in the holocaust survivor who trusts me, and in the hundred-year-old woman whose shoulders ache and who moves from cranky to serene, and in the friend whose heart is failing and whose humility shines in a radiant peace.

I see you in Andrzej and Mira, who never forget their immigrant origins, and whose compassion reaches around the world and is rooted in their beautiful home.

I see you in Kay, who has survived rape and come through as a recovering alcoholic and a wounded healer.

I see you in Denny, the iron marshmallow whose arguments seem predictably porous, but whose deeds are often magnificent.

I see you in friends with years of serene sobriety – emotional and physical – who know that all of us are powerless without our Higher Power, and who live one day at a time.

I see you in Father Casey's jokes, in his love for sixty years of parishioners, kids, couples struggling with their marriage, volunteer firemen and endless visitors to his last home – even on an ice-clad February Tuesday in upstate New York.

I see you in Margie, cerebral palsied, widowed, deaf, feisty, honest, often angry and in tears, but always full of faith, and laughing as hard as she cries.

I see you in the girls I taught – often not very well – who were crazed for the Beatles; I remember you in beautiful Laurie, an heiress who committed suicide in her twenties because she could not love herself, and her husband did not love her.

I see you in baby Jesse, nursing at his mom Claudia's breast.

I see you in Lourdes, stooping to harvest an acre of carrots, from 7 a.m. on Tuesday to 1 a.m. Wednesday.

I see you in Nana, who baked every afternoon and listened to us over four o'clock tea, sweetened with cookies and her kind gaze.

I see you in Señor Vargas, who labored from age twelve to fifty-eight, until he threw out his back lifting a marble slab on a construction job.

I see you in David, who loves our country even though the jungles of Vietnam are stamped on his soul, and who lives in enviable dependence on the Holy Spirit.

I see you in Elisabeth, who puts her many talents at the service of the "Y" so people of all ages and backgrounds can learn and grow.

I see you in Leo, reading aloud to a crowd, in English, about eternal love – even though he is not sure he believes in God.

I see you in Tom and Sharon, whose love for their kids and grandchildren is there in every season, through endless hours of coaching little league or tennis, and in bringing great food to family gatherings.

I hear you in the voice of my RSCJ sister, whose mind may be clouded with Alzheimer's, but whose heart speaks wisdom as she says: "It is not about fourteen ways of being perfect; it is about being grateful for receiving love, and passing it on. I am very happy."

I see you in Arturo and Mary and their girls, who in so many ways inspire and uplift others, and share the joy and faith of their Mexican-American culture.

I see you in Helen, who tells me that her life is about praying for other people.

I see you in Mark and Linda, proud of their four kids, in Linda whenever she laughs, and in Mark who weeps as he escorts his beautiful daughter down the aisle.

I hear you, Beloved, in Bach and Bert Bacharach, in Mendelsohn and Glenn Miller, in Sinatra and the Mormon Tabernacle Choir, in Pavarotti and Catherine Jennings, in Andrea Bocelli and in the purity of Gregorian chant and the ecstasy of Palestrina's polyphony. You are poetry beyond Emily Dickinson, science beyond astronauts, cosmic hero and victor in all actual and possible worlds, story beneath all sagas.

I seek you in the silence and solitude of simply breathing your presence, because without these, I would be blind and deaf to you in others, in your world, in your word.

I discover that you are consolation, because you never ask for perfection but only for a home in my fallible heart; only to pour out your love – your unfailing, personal, forgiving, passionately tender love. You are the tremendous lover in whom we may each make our home; you are the one who begs for room in the inn of every human heart.

You are willing to overcome any obstacle to transform me daily into "the bride of Amazement." (*When Death Comes*, Mary Oliver) ∽

A Long Conversation in My Heart

Barbara Quinn, RSCJ

What can I say about a lifelong friendship because, frankly, I can't remember when I didn't pray. As Mary Oliver writes in her essay, *Thirst*:

> *Oh Lord, I was never a quick scholar but sulked and hunched over my books past the hour and the bell; grant me, in your mercy, a little more time. Love for the earth and love for you are having such a long conversation in my heart. Who knows what will finally happen or where I will be sent, yet already I have given a great many things away, expecting to be told to pack nothing, except the prayers which, with this thirst, I am slowly learning.*

(*Thirst*, 69)

What to say about "such a long conversation in my heart".... Where to begin? Let me try.

I have always thought that prayer is similar to two people who fall in love and grow into their relationship over the years. At the beginning, the specifics of the relationship are crystal clear. They can remember where they met, what they talked about, what each was wearing and the expressions on the other's face. But now, with the passing of the years, the lines are blurred and the easy descriptions inadequate, while the intermingling of their lives, their hearts, are more real and rooted than anything else. They have become one as all the mystery and struggle and joy of their lives unfold. Life without the other is difficult to imagine.

It is something like that with my prayer. Our friendship has been going on for such a long time. Even when I was a child, God was a friend with whom conversation was easy and natural and constant. I prayed many a day walking home from school alone across a vast playing field or while skating on the frozen pond at the end of our street or, sure that my sister was sound asleep, slipping out of bed to kneel and talk with God before dropping off to sleep.

As I grew more intentional and more focused about my relationship with God, I was quite earnest and disciplined about learning how to pray as one "should." I suppose it was my version of getting the beginning rituals of a more mature relationship just right. As time moved along, I discovered all the ups and downs of any deep friendship: the initial glow and wonder, the unexpected disappointments and hurts, the slow revelation that this singular friend can be illusive and sometimes silent and clearly not prone to jump in and fix my questions and struggles. In fact, at times, I wondered if God heard at all.

Over the years, I have gradually come to believe that God is closer to me than my own skin; so close and so "all" that I cannot simply look outside myself for God, although God is as pervasive as the air we breathe, but that God – the Holy Community of Persons whose best name is Love – is deep within. Irish author Walter Mackin says it well:

> *The inside of you is like a well, a deep well about which you know very little. That must be your soul, where all the real things take place. And if it is a right deep place, and has been tended by your head, then he supposed God would be deep down in there whispering to you always about the realities. So that would be the real fair land, deep down in yourself.*

(*Seek the Fairland*, 299)

The long conversation in my heart with God has taught me gradually to face the "real" of my own deep well and the "real" of our world, both shot through with beauty and goodness and ugliness and even evil. Like the reflections in a crystal clear lake that mirror life as far as it can see, all the while opening into the depths beneath its surface, I have come to see that life is somehow all of a piece.

It is amazing to me how the language of God's Spirit within, like rumblings in an echo chamber, signals life or death, truth or deception, love or hate. Prayer is where I hear the soundings of God's Spirit as I listen to another and witness the deep goodness, the unrelenting longings, the quiet but incredible kindnesses, the courageous desires for hope and for love. It is where my idealistic heart aches because I can't believe we need to hurt one another as we do the world over.

Prayer is where I catch a glimpse of God's uncompromising love and so have the courage to name who I am when no one is looking. Prayer is where I hear the call to face life's realities as they are and to partner with God in deciding how to respond: to accept them as they are, to try to change them in some way, to let their reality change me. Prayer is where I sometimes catch a small glimpse of what God is like, this Holy Community of Persons, whether in the stillness of my room or in the sacred place of listening to another's heart or in the magnificence of nature as I take weekend walks around the reservoir. And when in India I experienced the beautiful interweaving of Hindu ritual with the Eucharist or holy hour, I knew again how big God is. My eyes often fill, and I am moved to silence as I touch and taste the Holy Mystery in all its awe and all its closeness.

I know, too, that sometimes my prayer is filled with silence. But now, unlike as in younger days when I wondered if God heard or cared at all, I have come to believe that God often works most powerfully in "secret" ways, in the quiet depths of my own being. Long ago, I read a book, *The Diary of a Country Priest* by George Bernanos, that powerfully influenced my sense of this. It is a beautiful tale of a sickly young priest, freshly ordained, who goes about his daily duties with no apparent success. If anything is outstanding it is his own sense of failure. Yet the reader is privy to the extraordinary impact of this young man day after day on country folk of all sizes and shapes, an impact, unbeknown to him. So steeped in God was he that his desire to love in whatever way he could opened him to know God's tender graciousness and constant presence. Even as he took his last breath, knowing that the suddenness of his death prohibited his receiving the last sacraments, he could utter the simple and profound meaning of his life: "Does it matter? Grace is everywhere." It was an early lesson for me that more than anything, God calls us simply to keep our eyes and hearts and actions fixed on God's love and God's ways and God will take over from there. I truly believe that.

And so the long conversation in my heart goes on. Growing in consciousness of this language of God's Spirit, learning to trust and surrender to the sure guidance of God's hopes for me and for our world, color how I see and what I hear and how I speak and where I walk. It is my prayer that the following article from our Constitutions kneads its way into my soul and the soul of the world more and more:

> *The Spirit dwelling within us*
> *gradually transforms us, enabling us*
> *through His power to remove whatever hinders His action.*
> *The Spirit unites and conforms us to Jesus*
> *and makes us sensitive to His presence*
> *within ourselves, in others and in all that happens.*
> *Thus we learn to contemplate reality*
> *and to experience it with His Heart,*
> *to commit ourselves to the service of the Kingdom*
> *and to grow in love:*
> *"Have this mind among yourselves*
> *which was in Christ Jesus"* (Philippians 2:5). § 21 ⁓

Faith, Love and Earnestness

Mary Patricia Rives, RSCJ

Once when Saint Madeleine Sophie Barat* was asked how to pray, she responded, "With faith, with love, and with earnestness." Praying with faith, with love and with earnestness is a way of life I have come to grasp over time in the Society of the Sacred Heart, but these attitudes were first taught to me as a child by my mother.

My mother was a woman filled with creativity, joy of life and a deep and boundless faith. I only realized later in life how profound and deeply rooted was her faith and trust in Our Lady who took her directly to Jesus and her God. For me, life was simple, family-oriented and filled with joy. Only looking back did I realize the challenges and tragedies my mother experienced living in Mexico City and Tampico, Mexico, especially because of the revolution in the twenties and thirties. With the revolution came the confiscation of all mineral rights, which personally touched my grandfather and our whole family. At the same time, there was a persecution of the Church that made living our faith so dangerous.

When I was four and my brother six, my father was killed. My uncle, the husband of my mother's only sister, was not well, and my grandfather was seriously ill. Good family friends advised my mother and aunt to leave the country for a while and travel to the nearest city in the United States, San Antonio, Texas. During the next three years, my uncle, grandfather and brother died. This is just a glimpse of what my mother faced, but she lived her life full of faith and trust that God would take care of us. When I reflect on this, I know that faith and love were and are deeply ingrained in me because of her.

At the same time, as I was growing up, my experience of church was of a rigid institution that taught it had the only truth in matters large and small and that was centered on the pious devotions that accompanied the liturgical year. My prayer consisted of daily Mass, vocal prayer and devotions. Very early, I began to question. I was influenced by school, friends and especially by provocative conversations. I began to awaken to my larger world. Then I met the Religious of the Sacred Heart.

My mother and aunt attended the Sacred Heart school in Mexico City, and my cousins attended Eden Hall and Overbrook in Philadelphia. My knowledge of the Society came only by hearsay until I was told that when I graduated from high school, I was going for another year of school to the Academy of the Sacred Heart, known as "The Rosary," in New Orleans. After that year in the boarding school, I chose to continue my studies with the RSCJs and asked to attend college at Grand Coteau.*

I knew there was much to experience and learn, and new worlds opened up for me during these years. Now my prayer was filled with new experiences and truths, and I slowly learned that I could find God in people, in events ... in all. Indeed, my prayer was becoming more personal, more inward, while at the same time more reaching out. A Jesuit chaplain at Grand Coteau had a profound influence on me. His liturgies were way ahead of the time, especially by including women in the rituals and inviting some to give homilies. At Grand Coteau I also began my journey of discovering the value of the present moment as my touch with reality.

Then I began to feel the call to religious life, though I kept saying to myself "not yet." I resonated with Francis Thompson's *The Hound of Heaven*:

> *I fled Him, down the nights and down the days;*
> *I fled Him, down the arches of the years;*
> *I fled Him, down the labyrinthine ways*
> *Of my own mind; and in the midst of tears*
> *I hid from Him, and under running laughter . . .*

Actually, I memorized the entire poem! During my years at the Rosary and Grand Coteau I discovered and witnessed the charism of the Society of the Sacred Heart. I saw lives of love lived daily with such joy. I was eager and willing to learn and in time to embrace that life. "Not yet" became "now."

Perhaps this is where the earnestness spoken of by Sophie came into play. I realized that I was seeking God and the real meaning of prayer. As a novice* one challenge for me came in being introduced to the Ignatian* method of meditation – writing points and placing myself in a time and setting in the life of Christ – a method that was not congenial to me. I started to question that so much of my life seemed to come with someone else's permission – how I prayed, what books I read, whom I could see, talk to or visit. My prayer began to be centered in trying to find the will of God in all this .... The best part was that I did keep my sense of humor and joy of life.

Over time I began to realize that it was the Spirit herself who was the one directing me. Vatican II came and much began to open up, even my prayer. I came to know that my life lived was prayer, was with God. I came to appreciate the Ignatian way of praying the gospels, though after being introduced to Eastern spirituality, I felt truly more at home in silence with God who truly knows and loves me. I have tried to take to heart the words of Jesus, "A new commandment I give to you . . . love one another as I love you." If God asks this of us, then to love each and every one must be possible. A fuller realization came to me in prayer: the essence of love is to share, and that is behind all creation, and that same love has been given to each one of us.

What is prayer? Prayer begins with faith, which I believe is a gift given in many ways. There are so many ways to look at this gift or to try to describe it. One incredibly beautiful path by which God introduces and helps faith to grow is through family and friends. Growth in faith is not an easy path as so much comes into play . . . time and place, where I grew up, went to school, choices I made, experiences that influenced my decisions, books I read, experiences of peace and joy, of sorrow, even of questioning the love of God. Each has a part to play in the beginning and growth of faith, which is the foundation of prayer; each has a part to play in the awareness of the truth that God is love and from that love in its essence is the desire to share. All has helped to form me to be the person I hope God wants me to be – daily to become more loving, more trusting, more generous . . . seeking and seeing God in all. "If you seek me you will find me, if you seek me with all your heart, I will let you find me." ∾

Let us be convinced that prayer and humility can triumph over the greatest obstacles and draw down the most signal graces.

—Saint Madeleine Sophie Barat

Spiritual Fitness

Diane Roche, RSCJ

It occurred to me recently, as I was trying to get in shape for what I knew was going to be a strenuous hike up a mountain, that prayer and physical exercise have a lot in common. I can join the gym, meet with a personal trainer to discover my strengths and weaknesses, buy the right clothes so I look the part; but unless I actually choose to show up faithfully over a period of time and let the machines do their work, I won't see any improvement in my cardio-vascular system, and I won't be able to make it up the mountain without hurting myself or even putting others at risk.

So, for me, prayer is all about a faithful practice. I simply get up early (usually 4:30 or 5:00), make a cup of coffee and go to my prayer corner, where I have a comfortable chair, the readings for the day and my journal. I spend the first few moments thinking about my dreams of the night before, sipping my coffee and being grateful for the first light outside my window. Then I take my time and read through the Scriptures and the reflections. Often there is something in the readings that triggers a memory or a desire to explore some emotional reaction in my journal. If not, I use the time to write down the main events of the previous day, particularly if there was a moment of either negative or positive energy. Finally, I put aside my coffee cup and my journal and allow my mind to rest quietly as I breathe in and out.

This period of time can last for fifteen or twenty minutes and is where I feel the real "work" of prayer happens. I consciously surrender any desire to make anything happen during this time, trusting instead that the one who sustains and calls me knows exactly what needs to be done. If I find myself swept away by a thought, I generally notice that my body has become un-centered as well, so I take a deep breath, correct my posture and focus on my breathing again, sometimes using a phrase to help me remember the flow of God's energy in and out of my body.

Occasionally as I feel my time of prayer coming to a close, specific people or situations will come to mind, and I allow myself to bring those persons into God's presence within me as I breathe in; and as I breathe out, I pray for peace or a release from suffering or for whatever seems needed.

During the rest of the day I try to integrate that same spirit into whatever unfolds. In particular I try to pay attention when I feel myself getting "un-centered" by some event, and to remember to take a conscious breath before I respond out of habit or compulsion in a way that would increase the suffering within or around me. Like most good things – vaccines, good policies, a healthy diet – the effects of this practice are subtle. While my failures to stay focused are obvious to me, other people are more likely to notice a change or make some positive observation.

It's a very humble, simple form of prayer that makes it extremely easy to adapt to the shifting requirements of community, work, travel and even physical limitations. As Angeles Arrien, a well-known psychologist and lecturer, pointed out, success in most things (including our prayer life) is mostly a matter of showing up, paying attention, being truthful and letting go. ∽

A genuine spiritual life compels us to breathe, live and move in God alone. Life, breath, action – that is the whole person. But let our living, breathing and doing be only for God, through Jesus Christ.

—Saint Madeleine Sophie Barat

Prayer Is My Whole Life

Pierina Ronconi, RSCJ

I get up at 4:00 a.m. and when I begin my prayer, I say: "Lord, let my prayer rise like incense to your presence in profound adoration and awe that you have raised this lowly creature to the summit of your love." After that I take the Bible and pray Psalm 121. Beautiful! After that, I pray Psalm145. I read only a portion because it is so long. Very beautiful. After that I pray the morning prayers in my *Give Us This Day* missal. Then the nurse comes in to help me dress. At about 5:35 I go to the chapel and pray the rosary. That way I ask Our Lady to keep me close to Our Lord. Then I do my spiritual reading before breakfast at 7:30.

My prayer is my whole life!

In the last period of my life, this image came to me: my tree of life. It stands erect and strong. Its roots are deep and spread out in the soil. This tree is losing its leaves one by one, and very few are still hanging on its branches. These, too, eventually will be falling.

I feel this tree is an image of my life, very well rooted in faith and in trust in my heavenly Father. He has become my confidant, as is my brother Jesus. There are not many friends anymore, no more letters arriving, but I never feel alone. I live in God's peace. Yes, I'm at the sunset of my life but there will never be complete darkness. My guardian angel – "Jeff" is the name I gave him – I feel his presence. I am at peace. What joy! ∼

The spirit of prayer is the soul of the soul and its life. God is in every sense the home of the soul and there only is our rest.

—Janet Erskine Stuart, RSCJ

Some Reflections on My Prayer in My 80s

Helen Rosenthal, RSCJ

Before I entered the Society of the Sacred Heart at nineteen, I talked to Jesus who was both a loving father and a good friend. I loved to make little visits to the Blessed Sacrament or drop into a church just to be with Jesus for a short conversation. I wanted to make up for all those who do not think of God or remember to thank God for being there for us.

When I entered the Society I was given the method of St. Ignatius to use for morning meditation. I was to prepare the hour of prayer each morning by choosing points from the gospels; we did not have meditation books. I seldom found the "points" helpful at 5:30 the next morning but learned to just let a phrase or an image from Scripture stay with me. This helped, and I remember one Lent, years later, when I spent the entire time with the agony in the garden. I could not move on until Good Friday.

Gradually my prayer became wordless. I developed a real relationship with each person in the Blessed Trinity during the five months so full of grace that I spent at our convent, the Trinità dei Monti,* in Rome. These relationships were a great gift before going to the motherhouse to prepare for final profession. Jesus taught me how to enter his Heart while I was at the Trinità. I had known from the beginning that I was called to go deep into the Heart of Jesus as the "solitude of His Heart was a crushing reality," words of Reverend Mother de Lescure that I have never forgotten.

Being sent directly from Rome to Chile without knowing any Spanish was a grace, and my prayer life reflected the missionary vocation that was such a gift for me. Our Lady was now very present to me in a concrete way; I had always loved her, but now her presence in my life became tangible. I found that I had a great desire to pray, and the more occupied I was in the school, studying at the same time, during the first years in Chile, the greater the longing just to be able to sit in silence with Jesus. I had some intense prayer experiences and also had a retreat at the end of my first year that was seven days of utter desolation, and then I woke up on the eighth day and was inspired to write all the joys that I experienced every day. When I showed this to my superior, she asked to keep it and sent it to the motherhouse; I am sorry that I did not keep a copy as I came to realize that for years the Lord had been calling me to serve God in joy. That desire deepens each year and has made gratitude one of the characteristics of my prayer.

How do I pray now? My prayer is a precious, sacred time that I love and desire, but it is a real hodge-podge of different things: reflection on the previous day, if I did not write my gratitude journal the night before; reading the gospel of the day; perhaps reading the pope's app or something sent by our mother general or the provincial to ponder, and then, hopefully, just sinking into silent prayer in the Heart of Jesus. Sometimes my thoughts run wild, but Jesus has taught me to just rest in his heart. Now we communicate without words. ∼

We learn to remain in silence
and poverty of heart before Him.
In the free gift of ourselves
we learn to adore and to abide in His love.

—Constitutions of the Society of the Sacred Heart §20

A Learning Experience

Marianne T. Ruggeri, RSCJ

Years ago, after spending the night with several ill students in the boarding school, I went to the chapel for morning meditation too exhausted to meditate or pray as I thought I should. As I knelt there, I realized that it was not what I did for Our Lord that was important at that time, but what Our Lord wanted to do for me. So I peacefully sat with the prayer, "Lord, take me as I am and make me what you want me to be."

Through the years, kneeling or sitting quietly with Our Lord continues to be one of my favorite ways of praying. Confident that God cannot refuse my request, I trust that Our Lord is with me, companioning me through the rest of the day. ﹏

"Give us thyself" is the best prayer we can pray, and "we give ourselves to thee" no better offering. For we do not know what to ask and what to offer. Leave it to him, but remember that we must mean to give all for all.

—Janet Erskine Stuart, RSCJ

Traveling a Lonely Road

Oonah Ryan, RSCJ

Since childhood I have had a growing sense of the presence of God, although in the course of many years, I went through some painful times when this sense was absent.

Twelve years ago I went through a time of enormous loss and pain, after which, for two years, I was blessed with a deepened and expanded awareness of God and in particular of Jesus in his suffering.

At the end of that time, during a thirty-day retreat* came a preview of what would happen in the years to come: an ever-increasing sense of an inner desert, physical pain, and a growing and more vivid sense of the power of evil. I'd been through batches of that stuff before, but the years since 2002 have been different. I often couldn't find the help I needed, and I began to know for the first time the demands of believing when one sees nothing, and I even wondered about a lot of realities I had taken for granted.

Bernadette Roberts, an American mystic, writes about the journey to no self in a way, for me, that Teresa of Avila and John of the Cross, who had for years been my guides, did not.

For some years, I have tried to pray for the world during the two or three hours in the middle of the night when I cannot sleep. I struggle to get to daily Mass. I just try to "never stop walking" – spiritually or physically.

I don't try to face inner darkness directly. I try to serve others in a busy, demanding ministry, and I know that more than ever, people are my way to God.

My poem, *Spirit Night*, reflects my experience of inner darkness

> *My spirit's cold, an empty winter building.*
> *There spiders stalk their prey.*
> *Surely the fire has gone out!*
> *It's a scary place to be*
> *walking in a shadow land between death and*
> *an old life that once had meaning.*

The Presence that used to haunt my very being
    at every moment of the night and day
    came by briefly, but it was different.
Powerful enough, poignant,
    and then it was gone.

I try to keep believing, but why and how?
Perhaps the Presence was but an illusion,
    an old longing for a god who's died.

Oh, indeed there may be a god,
but surely not the God I've known
and not the God that filled my youth,
    who pursued me so relentlessly.
Can that God even be?
Was it, she, he just a product of my longing,
    a filler of a space more empty than before?

Dark night . . . once I was secure in you.
Now walking barefoot on your rough and slippery stones,
    I can so easily stumble.
I fear in the lonely process of struggling through your maze,
    I've lost the guide, the friend I treasure.

Time creeps by on padded slippers.
Winter passes
Slowly spring dissolves, and summer comes.

A bent figure leans into the wind
    that blows from the river's edge.
He bids me draw near,
    and with old eyes able to see beyond the NOW
        speaks gently,
"Be still and wait, even though you hope not.
The One you have loved does not forget you, indeed knows well,
'To arrive where you are, to get from where you are not
you must go by a way wherein there is no ecstasy.'"[1]
Tears came, my eyes blurred, and when I looked again,
    The old man was gone.

---

1 T. S. Eliot: *Four Quartets*: "East Coker"

I have a few books that I turn to from time to time: the writings of the Rhineland mystic, Marguerite Porete; a book by several Dutch Carmelites, *In the Footprints of Love*; Scripture, of course; and the *National Catholic Reporter* for reflection on current church issues.

In these last ten years, it's often been hard to pray daily for two to three hours, especially at night, and then I sometimes have recourse to Scripture by drawing.

These drawings are not meant to be great art. They just come out of a need to focus and get rid of distractions, and out of my love of art, of images and nature. ∿

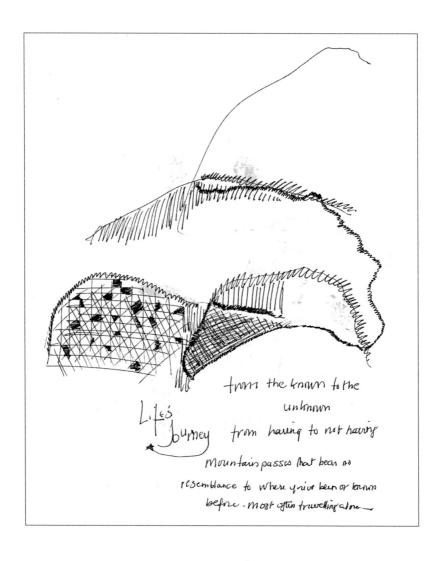

Coming to God as I Am

Mary R. Schumacher, RSCJ

During my retreat, it occurred to me that this is an appropriate time to reflect on prayer. Saint Paul encouraged us to pray always, and I am beginning to understand what this means to me. I am drawn to Jesuit spirituality, which is focused on finding God in all things, and I hope I perceive this happening as well.

Lately my formal prayer life has two forms: the prayer of technology and the Eucharist. Upon awakening in the morning, I usually sit on my patio and first experience the pink mountains as the sun rises. Nature had always drawn me into the presence of God. I grew up near Lake Michigan in Chicago and daily experienced the diversity of its movements and colors as I rode the bus to the Sacred Heart high school on Sheridan Road. Later, when I was teaching at Hardey Prep, the waves of the lake would restore my energy after a day of teaching grade school boys. I used to say, "My soul is in Lake Michigan." I love camping in nature as well and have made many retreats under the skies and on the rivers to discover the presence of God and God's unconditional love for me.

Then, after taking in God's beauty and the sunrise, I turn to my iPhone. Sometimes I read the headlines of the news of the day. This helps me get a global perspective on what needs prayer in our world. Then I listen to the Scripture of the day with the application *Pray As You Go*. There are several other ways that I focus my day: I read a saying from the calendar of Janet Erskine Stuart* or Sophie* or a grief recovery book. Sometimes I share the fruit of my morning prayer by texting a friend about some of what has happened.

At other times, I may watch a pertinent YouTube video that helps me prepare for a retreat or for spiritual direction. Music is often helpful for me and for my prayer as well. YouTube provides beautiful photography to go with many religious songs.

Then I usually attend the Eucharist in the morning. I listen again to the Scripture that directs me to a word to live out for the day. It is here that I bring those people in my life who particularly need prayer. I always ask for God's help at the consecration and renew my vows after communion.

Throughout the day I attempt to find God in all my encounters with others. In the evening I reflect on where I've missed the mark and promptly admit it, if possible. Evening prayer is often more peaceful and an expression of gratitude.

Recently I attended the Janet Erskine Stuart* conference in London. Two things have struck me about her life of prayer. The first thing is how grief shaped her spirituality. On account of the death of her mother when Janet was just fourteen months old, and of her caretaker half-sister, Theodosia, when she was nineteen, Janet was always searching for meaning and truth throughout her life. She had an empty vulnerability that impelled her forward, seeking God to fill this void.

Janet Erskine Stuart also struggled between the head and the heart in her prayer life. She, like all RSCJs, was trained in Ignatian spirituality* and meditation, including the familiar three points of Scripture for our prayer. Then Janet turned more to imaginative and contemplative prayer. Perhaps this is a process of prayer to which we can all relate. She was a holistic person and a model of spirituality for the twentieth century.

In the end, perhaps we all just need to come to God as we are. Our prayer is what it is, and it is important not to compare our prayer with others or feel our prayer is lacking. We are personally loved by God as God's children and called by name. Each one of us has a unique, personal relationship with our Creator.

The struggle of another oftentimes touches my prayer life. Recently, I have been on a journey with a person who is experiencing deep grief, and I wrote this poem about bridges for her:

Bridges

Our journey through life
Experiences many highs and lows,
Mountains and valleys
Joys and tears

And across every bridge we grow in depth, desire, and wisdom.
As our hearts are wounded, pruned, and loved.
We enter the bridge with trepidation and hope
Wondering how long it will take,
To journey to the other side.

Trusting in our past experience
We continue along the bridge of the unknown, as we come
To a new center of our being.
Our being loved and cared for

Allows us to become more loving, trusting, and caring.
Out of this bridge and transition
I will discover once again
Who I am and how
The journey has prepared me for
A new destination.

Life's many bridges
Call us forth
And lead us in new directions
To travel in ways
Of loving kindness
Toward others and ourselves. ❧

Moving Forward in Life through Prayer

Patricia Shaffer, RSCJ

I have had some wonderful experiences in my life of prayer.

In 2004, Thich Nhat Hahn, known to his followers as Thay, meaning teacher, gave a presentation at the University of San Diego, where I taught. There were more than 4,000 attendees, and I made certain that I sat by myself, not with friends, so that I could take it all in without the distraction of conversation. It was a very moving experience. This was a time when teaching and research were a heavy weight on my shoulders. I needed to learn Thay's way of praying, of breathing in and knowing "that the only person I can change is myself...." I took all of this in and tried to live it. My spiritual director gave me a series of recordings using Thay's prayer. For more than five years I continued to use what I learned about mindfulness and prayer.

While reading Sister Phil Kilroy's *Life of St. Madeleine Sophie Barat*, I came upon a quote I found helpful: "Unite solitude to the work we do and counter this whirlwind with a deep cavern where the soul can take refuge as often as possible. For us this cavern in the rock is the Heart of Christ." This led me to a new way to pray in the face of my stressful ministry.

Then I turned to the life of Janet Erskine Stuart* and was so impressed by her gift of herself to the Society. I was touched by her desire to visit almost all of the provinces* of the Society and her extensive travels. She solidified the Society's internationality. This gift of herself left its mark on me. In prayer, I gave myself to God, just as Mother Stuart had, despite the pressure of ministry.

Now I am learning to let go. After decades at the University of San Diego, I am ending my involvement with many organization, especially science connections and university organizations (chemistry department, Founders Club, etc.). I was given Richard Rohr's book, *Immortal Diamond, The Search for the True Self*, and have pondered it.

> The diamond was first made by another, and it is indeed drawing us forward into a brilliance that is now uniquely ours. Could this be what we are really doing when we say we are praying for someone?

Yes, we are holding them in our heart space. Do it in an almost physical sense, and you will see how calmly and quickly it works. Now the Sacred Heart and the Immaculate Heart have transferred to you. They are pointing for you to join them there. The 'sacred heart' is then your heart too.

This is what Father Rohr calls converting the head into heart.

Very recently, what has helped me most in prayer is a quote from Etty Hillesum that appeared in an essay by Mariola Lopez Villanueva, RSCJ, in our province's *Heart* magazine (Spring 2013, 16):

> This hour of silence is not easy. It must be learned: to dislodge our noisiness, including our emotions and edifying thoughts and to convert the deepest part of ourselves into a vast empty plain into which not even the slightest trace of malice impedes something of God or of love from entering.

Mariola adds:

> We need so much this silencing and space for love! Without this deepening, without going down to this place in the heart, we cannot keep up hope in a world that is so fragmented and violent, nor can we discover and celebrate how much beauty and goodness lies hidden in it.... We need to return to the interior Master who waits for us within and allow him each day to train us in silence and simplicity. Exposed to his presence, we can abandon ourselves to his mystery.

Once I have been converted to "his Mystery," I turn to the liturgy of the day, especially the psalm of the day (sometimes using *Psalms for Praying* by Nan C. Merrill). I reflect on the gospel or on the first reading, whichever is more moving to me. Since we received *Life Unfolding, Offering the Gift** several years ago, I ponder something taken from the sections on community, interior life or living a simple life.

Community
Certain factors in the world "invite us to discern new ways of relating, because we live the gospel not only through our apostolic actions, but also through the gratuitous gift of ourselves to each other in community."

Interior life
Our incarnational spirituality flows from our deep relationship with Jesus. We see the link between this experience of Jesus and our own way of living and growing in

relationship with others. Our contemplative life is what helps us to discover God's love in the wounds of the world. We need to be transformed so that we may glimpse the face of Christ in the faces of the poor and in one another.

Simple life

Within the context of today's world, we feel called to deepen our commitment to the poor and to reflect on the way we live and how we understand our vow of poverty. We hear from Jesus a renewed call drawing us toward the marginalized, the fragile, the excluded, and those who lack the basic necessities of life, inviting us to collaborate with those who put their energies at the service of the Kingdom.

I did not want to retire, leave San Diego and come to Oakwood.* So Mariola's article in *Heart* and our gift in *Life Unfolding* helped me through prayer to move forward in love for others. ❧

Let us hand over our cares to Jesus, praying that he will act for us. Then everything will take care of itself.

—Saint Madeleine Sophie Barat

Steps in a Labyrinth

Regina Shin, RSCJ

Prayer is personal, private and sacred for me, so to share how I pray seems like sharing a secret out loud. Prayer is being, being with my inner self and being with God. It is trying to reach the center of God, like taking steps towards the center of a labyrinth.

Art has been a primary medium of my prayer. Often, the layers of color block paintings by Mark Rothko or the photo images produced by Cindy Sherman grab my attention quickly without any "filtering" and invite me directly to a deeper level without much effort.

Or I make art myself.

Sometimes I take my camera, especially a film camera, and walk around either a breath-taking, beautiful, inspiring place or an area which stirs me up with many, many questions.

Sometimes, I try to express images that I experience by drawing, painting, or by any means – jotting down words, fragmented phrases, typing, doodling, using electronic methods. Either gazing at an art piece or making the artwork invites me directly to enter into the "core" or heart of my soul. A similar experience, for me, is centering prayer*, but art requires much less effort.

This process to me is indescribable with words, but it creates in me a "being" or sensing in a well of peace. This is all I can describe with words. I seek to integrate my prayer with my daily life and hope my daily life will reflect my life of prayer – loving, kind, balanced, open and mindful of beauty. ∿

Several Sacred Ways of Prayer

Sheila Smith, RSCJ

Praying has been a big part of my life since I was a child. However, because prayer is a relationship, it takes many different forms and meanings at various moments along life's journey. In this reflection, I will write about four of the ways in which praying is currently part of my life. I will conclude with a short reflection on images of God in prayer.

My primary work at this time is to write a doctoral dissertation in theology. During this writing process, I find two ways of praying particularly helpful. The first I describe as "praying my writing and writing my praying." Having the time to study and write is a privilege that feels sacred to me. Although very intellectual, writing as praying and vice versa involves a process of intense listening with the heart, inner transformation, self-understanding, expression and active participation in an academic community. As a middle-aged woman, I am discovering anew and honing the unique aspect of God's mission to which I am called and for which I am most challenged and gifted.

Perhaps because my work is so academic, a second way of praying that I currently practice is less intellectual and reflective. I refer to contemplation. In hindsight, my first experiences of contemplative prayer happened during childhood when I was filled with a deep sense of wellbeing while outdoors surrounded by trees or beside the river. This sense of wellbeing I now also understand as oneness with God. In my early twenties, I often felt myself enter into contemplation while praying the rosary or during eucharistic adoration. Now, I am also drawn into stillness and oneness through contemplation following prayerful body movement, such as simple breathing and relaxation exercises. Resting in God through contemplation is grounding, centering and energizing.

It has recently become important for me in my practice of contemplation to join others. One way I do this is to belong to the RSCJ *Cor Unum* meditation group. Members use Insight Timer, an application for phone, computer or tablet to join the open group. Every day, when each one contemplates or meditates, she can see that many others are praying throughout the world, and which of those are also members of *Cor Unum*.

Less frequently practiced, but exceedingly significant on my faith journey, is a third way of praying, that I practice through "touch drawing." Although this is a form of creative expression that can be practiced for many purposes, for me it is a way of praying. Touch drawing, like journaling, is a creative way to touch God's life and love stirring within. I find this way of praying to be particularly helpful during times of fear or darkness. Touch drawing allows me to bring feelings about life's experiences to expression outside of myself so as to listen more deeply to God. Sometimes, I discover in a series of drawings a pattern or a story that is helpful in moving through times of darkness or discernment.

Also important for me, especially during intense moments of discernment, annual retreats,* and also in times of darkness, is a fourth way of praying: dreaming and dream analysis. I have a devotion to the biblical dreamers: Joseph, son of Jacob in the Hebrew Bible, and Joseph the father of Jesus in the Christian Bible. I often pray to them before sleeping to awaken me to God's presence in the dream world. Working with night dreams, as a way of listening to God in one's life, can be an incredible experience of awe at the amazing, intimate ways that God loves, challenges and acts in our lives. Analyzing my dreams has helped me to work through times of pain, grief, confusion and doubt. It has also affirmed my desires, choices and human development.

Finally, I would like to share something about images of God in relation to the ways of praying mentioned above. As a member of a congregation dedicated to the Sacred Heart, Love is my most cherished image of God. Two expressions of the Sacred Heart of Jesus are prominent for me at this moment on my journey. They are Shekinah and Counselor. Shekinah denotes for me the divine presence of Love that I know, feel and need dwelling within the temple of my being. Counselor describes God's gazing, listening, holding, empowering presence that I know, feel and need surrounding me. To need and to be supported by God through these images of the Sacred Heart, as I do my part in God's mission, unites me to Philippine Duchesne,* named *Quahkah-kanumad* ("the woman who prays always") by the Potawatomi, and to all the praying women upon whose shoulders I stand. ☙

This contemplative attitude permeates our whole being,
helping us to live ever more united to Christ
in our relationships, our tasks and our ministry;
it becomes a powerful force of conversion and transformation
for mission.

—Constitutions of the Society of the Sacred Heart §22

Wait, Listen

Anne Sturges, RSCJ

For me, prayer is
choosing to spend time in,
asking to be somehow aware of,
the union that already exists,
that is a gift (that is his gift).
A candle flame his love for me.
I challenge myself, "Wait, listen."

I sit on my bed, legs out straight.
They do not move.
My hands do move, however,
as does my fickle mind.
I begin with words learned long ago:
"I come to you to take your touch before I begin my day."
"Your touch" is then my mantra.

I close the hour with other words from a retreat:
"I take to my heart the assurance
of your comradeship, my friend."
A note on my bed all day reminds me
"Wait, listen." ∿

Drawn in God's Footsteps

Mary Jane Sullivan, RSCJ

As I look back now in my eighties, I notice that God has drawn me in patterns that are similar over my lifetime. Basically, then, my prayer is the action of God in me. I have not always recognized this, but for some reason I remember from the days we chanted the Office* in Latin a quote: *Trahe me, post te curremus, in odorum unguentorum tuorum.* "Draw me in your footsteps. Let us run" (Song of Songs 1:4).

Over the years in parishes, I often taught short courses in prayer, opening up several different ways of prayer so that each one might find the way(s) for her. I'd begin with awareness of being in God's presence. Then *lectio divina,** centering prayer* and Ignatian contemplation* were those I focused on most. I told the folks that each day as I began my time of prayer, I asked, "How shall I pray today?" However, in the summer of 2009 after my retreat in Joigny,* I went to visit Saint Madeleine Sophie* in Paris. The *châsse* containing her body had recently been moved from Belgium to a church in Paris near the house where she died. I had about an hour before Mass was to begin. When I asked, "How shall I spend this hour?" I heard deep within, as from Sophie, "You never need to ask that question again." That gift keeps giving each day as I learn to let Jesus draw me into Abba.

A particular help over the past several years has been a suggestion from a Jesuit director of my retreat. He suggested that on the last day of the retreat in the evening I write a love letter to Jesus before going to bed. In the morning I was to let Jesus write a love letter to me. These are some of the deepest experiences of my life, and continue to be effective in my prayer today.

As I write this reflection on my prayer, I want to conclude with overwhelming gratitude for God's drawing me these many years. ～

*Our one passion should be the love of Christ
and the desire to make him loved.*

—Saint Madeleine Sophie Barat

Prayer without Boundaries

Stephany Veluz, RSCJ

Prayer is always a coming home experience. I find my prayer in Micah's famous line of what is asked of Israel: "to do right, to love goodness, and to walk humbly with your God." Prayer is living life in the solitude of my heart as well as in generous service for another in the heart of the community and ultimately in the Heart of God.

My prayer is quite simple. I come home to God in my breath. As I do so I notice the thoughts, and so I breathe in God's life and exhale what needs to be let go of. Sometimes it is inhaling deeply the refreshing tenderness of God in the growing silence of my consciousness. It is exhaling a loving-kindness prayer for someone and/or for the people of the world. At other times, it is inhaling my deep need for healing and exhaling a longing desire for God.

Sometimes I ponder a text in Scripture, starting with reflection and meditation, but always ending in the quiet, grace-filled Presence of the Trinity. Listening, sharing, listening more . . . .

I do appreciate the palpable energy that may come during prayer. But this gift is rare. I am simply filled with peace and gratitude each time – to know deeply in my heart the consciousness that God is there for me and for each one in the world. I walk with the consciousness of the Mystery of God each moment, and it is enough. As I grow closer and more trusting, I realize even more the unconditionality of God's love and the expansiveness of God's mercy. Yes, my illusions, fantasies and self-absorption are revealed with gentleness. I see this small self in the Heart of God forgiven and blessed. I see the world in there, too – broken like me – and lavished with grace. And so all in all, God becomes more the Center.

Prayer now has no boundaries. I breathe in God's life and that God-life enables me to be . . . and to be life as well for another, trusting that Christ is manifested and glorified in all that I am and in all that I do.

I am older now, and this kind of prayer has nourished me for many years. It has helped me immensely to come home to God and to myself. I tried other forms and techniques when I was younger; they were helpful then. Does it really matter how we pray, or the techniques we use? I have come to appreciate that in prayer what truly matters is who I am becoming, and with whom I am in relationship. The God of Mystery, of Love and of Compassion is ever present and ever faithful. I am blessed, and I ask Mary to lead me to her Son more and more so that I might magnify God all my life as she did.

Finally, prayer is letting God delight in me. As I do so, I learn to delight in God and the life God continues to lavish on me so generously. ∽

Prayer, the contemplative outlook on the world,
union with Christ in daily living
make us grow in the interior life,
so that in all circumstances we seek
to glorify the Heart of Jesus.

—Constitutions of the Society of the Sacred Heart §23

A Prayer Evolving

Deanna Rose von Bargen, RSCJ

I have tried many types of prayer during my lifetime, not necessarily through choice or decision, but usually because I have been drawn this way or that, and prayer seems to have just evolved over time.

I was going to say that no one taught me my first mode of prayer, when I was a child and a teenager. However, I do believe that the Sisters of Saint Joseph of Carondelet, who taught me as a child, encouraged us to make visits to the Blessed Sacrament in the parish church next door. There I simply "talked with Jesus." I grew up in a Jesuit parish in Lewiston, Idaho, where devotion to the Sacred Heart and statues and paintings of the Sacred Heart were almost an everyday experience. My maternal grandmother had a huge reproduction of a painting of the Sacred Heart and one of Mary, equal in size, hanging on her bedroom wall, and I saw these images often. So, Jesus was always "about heart" and "about love" and "about suffering." Also, I was aware that my grandmother walked to daily morning Mass even in snowy weather. I could tell that prayer meant a lot to her. I also enjoyed going into our parish church after dark, when only the red sanctuary lamp was glowing, and having "heart to heart" chats with Jesus present in the Blessed Sacrament in the darkened church. I heard my calling there. In the eighth grade I chose Catherine of Siena for my confirmation saint, because I thought it was so very cool that she had "traded hearts with Jesus."

I continued to pray in this way at the San Diego College for Women, where yearly retreats were preached by Jesuits. In the noviceship* we were all taught the Ignatian* form of prayer whereby one put oneself into a gospel scene, imagining oneself as a part of a particular story. This method definitely strengthened my relationship with Jesus, in spite of the almost rigid step-by-step way that it was presented.

With simplified variations, I continued praying in this way until my early forties, when I made a retreat with two Indian RSCJs who combined prayer with yoga. I had already had a course on eastern religions and began to realize that there were deep waters in Hindu and Buddhist styles of prayer/meditation. I do not even know or remember how I prayed for the next twenty years – but once I began yoga, I have never quit. I do know that prayer became quieter and gradually more wordless. I didn't ask for anything, but just tried to be present. I grew more and more reflective as well as receptive.

When I moved back to Idaho at age sixty-one to care for my mother, I connected with the Benedictine Sisters at Cottonwood, Idaho, made retreats there, and participated in their most lovely method of singing and reciting the Divine Office.* It was very "slowed down" and prayerful. During retreats there, I often needed nothing else but that prayer twice a day, plus mindful walks through the woods and among the wildflowers and precious cattle of my childhood summers. (I love cows!) Mindfulness had become very important to me, having read Thich Nhat Hanh's book, *The Miracle of Mindfulness*.

Though I had heard the term before and thought I knew what centering prayer* was (breathing and relaxing, I thought), I really didn't know what it was until one day I reconnected with my former teacher from Catholic grade school. She simply asked me if I practiced centering prayer. I asked her, "What is it, exactly?" From that moment (I was sixty-five years old), I delved into John Main's and Thomas Keating's books with a vengeance! My spiritual director also clarified for me exactly what was meant by *lectio divina*,* and so I started consciously praying that way, too. I think I was already doing *lectio divina* without even knowing that is what it was called. I had so overdosed on spiritual books in my twenties that I had quit reading spiritual books altogether for quite a number of years, and so I missed knowing the labels for various forms of prayer.

I am now in my seventies, and I know no other way to pray than centering prayer. There are no more "lightning strikes" or feelings of great consolation, but sometimes — notice that I say "sometimes" — only a deep and quiet peace and awareness of oneness with God. I am writing this without even knowing what I mean by it all. I have learned to give distractions little attention, though I do get a bit peeved upon discovering that, once in a while, the entire prayer time was distracted. (This most often happens when I forget to say my repetitive mantra; I usually follow John Main's advice in this, saying the mantra beginning to end). I also continue the yoga.

At the beginning of the prayer time and at its conclusion, I make sure my heart is in it, and that I am conscious of what I am about to do or have just finished doing. It would be so easy for me to engage in daily prayer in a mechanical way, because of so many things on my daily agenda. Then I could just "tick it off" as an accomplishment before moving on to the next item of the day. Instead, I find that this conscious attempt to remind myself of what I am about to do or have just finished doing, is helpful for getting my priorities straight and then for moving into the rest of the day. (I guess I should listen to what I tell my adult students, that it's all about the first commandment!)

Between the end of the morning prayer time and that of the next morning, I often experience a longing for the next time. I often wonder why, since there are no more fireworks or great insights in this type of prayer.... I teach with great conviction that God longs for us, so maybe I should pay attention here....

So, yes, my prayer has changed over time. Other forms of prayer continue to intrigue me. Maybe, someday....

*Each religious finds her own rhythm of prayer
and will decide how best she is to be faithful
to what Christ asks of her and of the Society,
discerning the method and style of her prayer-life.*

—Constitutions of the Society of the Sacred Heart §25

Signs of God's Fingerprints

Anne Wachter, RSCJ

Sometimes when I am praying I am absolutely silent and still – completely unaware of any stimulus. Sometimes I put my pen in my non-dominant left hand, and have a conversation with God – somehow the switch allows the essential to bubble up. I listen to music and read and contemplate Scripture – both can be instructive and moving.

Sometimes I'm just outdoors, caught by God in nature. The moon does not produce light, it reflects light... all around us, there are signs of God's fingerprints, lessons and reflections of the deeper reality of our lives, of our call.

Truth is something I can only touch from limited perspective. Writing poetry is one way I enter this reality. Prayer is an invitation, poetry my expression.

Here are four examples:

Scrounging for a Living

She glances and digs . . . double checks each blue bin with her little yellow gloves protecting her hands, an oversized coat hanging down....

Deborah is her name, I think.

Two hours ago she made her way up the street, collecting cans and bottles, scraping a living or just obsessed with squirreling away every redeemable penny. Dr. Pepper – intuition, the spirit or serendipity as she calls it . . . we connected.

I see her with regularity – now.

She was invisible to me until she helped my sister find her way home.

Mystery, hunch, – connected.

The importance of weekly recycling!

For what do I glance, dig, and double-check . . . with regularity?

Crystal Morning

The earth rests –
  deep in sleep beneath
  layer upon layer
  of ice and snow.
  Again,
  the air is filled with snow
    each flake
  peacefully
  making its way to
  add
    yet another
  dimension of white
  to this wonderland of
    silence
  where
  the earth is renewed in the
    darkness
  below
  its thick blanket.
Yesterday, today, tomorrow –
  the frozen moisture is
relentless
    in its presence –
    persistent, steady and oh (!)
    so very beautiful.

January –
in her finest dressing gown –
  extravagant and
perfect
  to the last drip
of ice
    off
the tiniest of branches
and berries,
encased in
frozen wonder.

Yet – yet – it snows –
still more whiteness –
the earth sleeps, and
hope is a flame, burning in the
heart
of this mystical winter wonderland.
I am grateful to be able to sit and
  to listen to the
  rhythmic breathing of
  the earth at rest
  and the air as she
    whispers knowingly
of the presence of
    THE INFINITE.

Truth shall spring from the Earth

Truth springs from the Earth . . .
as fish splash mightily . . .
        seeking food and getting
tangled in overhanging lakeside trees & bushes
        or lily pads out a ways.
A heron takes flight over the water
in the distance, horses neigh . . . birdsong and
chirping competitions fill the air.
Far off, the drone of civilization can be discerned.

        The rising sun pulls the morning mist
                skyward
        rays of eternity show the path
                no resistance —
        a gentle, steady return —
                the Spirit reclaims in the
        light what had descended
                in the night
        it happens every day
        Truth springs from the Earth.

Arise, my beloved, and come!

Ah, you are beautiful!
With great delight, I have called you
    forth from the shadows of sinfulness,
    of brokenness, of alienation, of rejection.
I have gathered you at my banquet table
to nurture you, to feed you, to slake your thirst.
My hand rests upon you. My arms embrace you.

Arise, my beloved, and come!

The winter of struggle is past.
Flowers spring forth in the earth.
Your time of homecoming is now.

See my face.
Hear my voice.
You are mine and I am yours.

As dawn becomes day,
    as day becomes dusk,
    as dusk becomes darkness.
I seek you
    I hold you
    I will not let you go.

You bring gladness to my heart.
I am ravished by your glances
You are my beloved and I greatly desire you.

Arise, my beloved, and come!

I set myself as the seal upon your heart.
My love for you is stronger than death.
My passion for you is unquenchable.

I wait to warm you by the fires of my mercy.
I wait to wash you in the sea of my compassion.
I wait to anoint you with the oil of gladness.

Arise, my beloved, and come!

I dwell with you as a good gardener.
You stroll the earth as my companion.
You are my voice, you are my heart. ⤳

Letting the Spirit Pray in Me

Mary Pat White, RSCJ

Over the years in my work with university students, I often heard: "I want to pray but I don't know how." One can always teach some methods of prayer like *lectio divina*,* the Ignatian method* of meditation and centering prayer,* which many people, myself included, find very helpful. But in the end I have to admit I really don't know how to pray either. Nevertheless, I'm drawn by our charism* and our spirituality that hold out this great ideal of "being wholly contemplative, whole apostolic."

At this moment in time, for me, prayer begins with my walk up the Berkeley hills first thing in the morning. Because it's early, generally there is a fog that envelops the hills and houses and sometimes even swirls around me. I surrender myself to the delicious silence that it creates and try not to lose my focus, which happens so readily when I begin to think of the day ahead and, well, all sorts of things.

My favorite place to settle is the prayer space I've created in my room where I have a singing bowl, incense burner, candle, a labyrinth plaque and other small objects that pull me into a "mood" for prayer. What I'm trying to do is prepare myself for quiet and the gentle awareness of God's presence that will come if I don't block it with all my "ego stuff" that can easily get in the way. Sometimes reading the Scriptures of the day and other favorite sources moves me away from the everyday anxieties that frequently haunt me when I sit down to pray. This practice helps me to perceive whatever it is differently, and points me toward what I'm really about, my real goal, each morning during this sacred time.

I pay attention to my posture. I let myself become aware of my breathing, and then I try to control it a bit by deepening and lengthening each inhalation and exhalation. This seems to help me let go of the distractions and go downward and inward into the interior quiet. It is especially at this point that I really know that I don't know how to pray! I realize that all I can do is set the stage and try to make myself available to God and be intentional about letting God transform me through an outpouring of love. It will then be my responsibility to share that love throughout the day.

This quote from Richard Rohr, OFM, speaks well to this:

I don't know how to talk to you, God. I don't know
who you are. I don't know how to look for your face.
But don't look at me. Just look at your Son.

—*Eucharist as Touchstone*

And, here, I paraphrase his thought in a way that works for me. "Look at the Heart of your Christ. I'm with him. He is my friend, my beloved, my love. He is my prayer. Listen to him." And I remind myself, "He is praying in and through me."

Catherine of Siena references this experience when she says: "My 'me', my 'me' is God." And also, "I remember that moment when I knew, and knew that I knew, that God was in me and I was in God."

How long one stays in this place of silence with focused attention probably doesn't matter all that much, or even if my experience is more like being on an inner see-saw. I am sure that it is the desire, the true longing of the heart and not the weakness of my efforts that God notes. And so, when I draw the prayer to a close it is with the intention to return to this place throughout the day in, at least, nano-seconds, to this place in my heart and God's, carved out by God's prayer, not mine. ❧

When one loves God, one never says, "Enough."

—Saint Rose Philippine Duchesne

Glossary

Adoration, night adoration
A period of silent prayer, usually before the Blessed Sacrament; night adoration was generally possible only in houses of formation where there were sufficient novices to replace each other throughout the night.

Adoro Te
"I adore you," a Latin eucharistic hymn written by Saint Thomas Aquinas in 1264.

Asanas
Traditional yoga prayer postures accompanied by attentive breathing

Barat, Saint Madeleine Sophie (1779-1865)
Founder of the Society of the Sacred Heart in post-revolutionary France; superior general for sixty-three years; dedicated the order to making God's love known, especially through education. At her death there were over 3,000 religious and 110 foundations on four continents. She was canonized in 1925.

Candidate
Someone testing her vocation to religious life by living with a community; once called a "postulant"

Centering Prayer
A form of contemplative prayer which emphasizes interior stillness, sometimes accompanied by a sacred word, for example, "Jesus," "Lord," "Love"

Charism
From the Greek, meaning gift; a word used by religious orders to refer to the particular, freely given gift of God entrusted to the community for the sake of the world; the RSCJ *charism* is to make God's love known.

Christ Pantocrator
A Greek title given to Christ meaning "all-powerful," with the added nuance of his active involvement in bringing his purposes to fruition; captured perfectly in Col 1:15-17

Christian Meditation
The name given to a variation of centering prayer promoted by John Main, OSB (1926-1982), founder of the ecumenical World Community of Christian Meditation

Circular Letter

Written by the superior general of the Society of the Sacred Heart, the letter developed a particular spiritual theme and was circulated among RSCJs across the world.

Constitutions of the Society of the Sacred Heart

The official document that brings a community into being, containing the ideals and norms for living as a vowed Religious of the Sacred Heart through various stages of formation, in various ministries, and in diverse settings

1815: The Constitutions of 1815 contain the original vision of Saint Madeleine Sophie Barat.

1982: The Constitutions of 1982, prepared in light of the Second Vatican Council's call for *aggiornamento,* or "updating," of religious life. The Society of the Sacred Heart made the decision not to try to amend Saint Madeleine Sophie's document, but to bind it together with a newly articulated vision, faithful to her thinking but accommodated to the contemporary world.

Cor unum et anima una in Corde Jesu

Motto of the Society of the Sacred Heart, "One Heart and One Soul in the Heart of Jesus;" shorthand reference, *cor unum,* refers to the Love which binds the Sacred Heart family together

Devise (see probation)

Divine Office (see Liturgy of the Hours)

Duchesne, Saint Rose Philippine (1769-1852)

Born in Grenoble, France, Philippine met Madeleine Sophie Barat in 1804, and became an RSCJ under her tutelage. In 1818 she and four companions brought the Society to the New World, where Philippine longed to work with Native Americans; the Potawatomi tribe named her the woman-who-prays-always. She was canonized in 1988.

Examen

A prayerful reflection on the events of the day to discern God's presence and become more responsive to God's desires. Steps include thanksgiving, prayer for light, a look back through the day, gratitude or sorrow as appropriate, a look ahead, concluding prayer.

General Chapter

Highest governing body of the Society, including provincials, district and area superiors, elected delegates and *ex officio* members; this international meeting convenes every eight years.

Chapter 2000 theme: "Our educational mission: a pathway to discover, a place to announce the love of the Heart of Jesus"

Chapter 2008 theme: "RSCJ Spirituality: Dialogue around the Fire, Candle, Well, Meal ..."

Chapter documents: the deliberations and conclusions of the Chapter, published for dissemination throughout the Society

Give Us This Day

A monthly prayer booklet containing, among other features, the prayers and readings of each day; a shared resource available to every RSCJ and Associate of the United States – Canada Province; published by Liturgical Press

Grand Coteau College

At one time in its history (1939-1956), the school at Grand Coteau was both an academy and an accredited four-year college.

Ignatius, Ignatian

Saint Ignatius of Loyola (1491-1556), founder of the Society of Jesus (Jesuits); author of *The Spiritual Exercises* which contains numerous meditative exercises; RSCJs were formed in the Ignatian pattern of meditation.

Janet Erskine Stuart (see Stuart)

Joigny, France

Birthplace of Saint Madeleine Sophie Barat, ninety miles south east of Paris; her family home is now a retreat center.

Kenwood

Established in Albany by Mother Aloysia Hardey on the Rathbone property in 1859, Kenwood was an academy, a house of formation before 1969, and an infirmary before it closed in 2008.

Lectio divina

Monastic in origin, this pattern of "divine reading," usually of a text of Scripture, moves from reading to meditation to prayer and contemplation.

Life Unfolding – Offering the Gift
> Published in 2013; the fruit of a meeting, held in Guadalajara, Mexico, to discuss initial formation, focused on formation as a lifelong process; identified community, interior life and simplicity as priorities for today

Liturgy of the Hours
> The common prayer of the Church, once called the Divine Office; primarily composed of psalms and canticles, and prayed at various hours of the day; the Little Office of Our Lady, a simplified variant of the Liturgy of the Hours, was sung in choir by RSCJs until the reforms in religious life and in the liturgy following Vatican II. Foremost hours include *Lauds* (morning prayer), *Vespers* (evening prayer) and *Compline* (night prayer).

Madeleine Sophie Barat (see Barat)

Magnificat
> A word meaning "magnifies," the *Magnificat* is Mary's song of praise found in Luke 1:46-55; it begins "My soul magnifies the Lord; my spirit rejoices in God my Savior."

Novice
> Following a year of candidacy, a newcomer spends two years learning the way of life of the community before asking to make first vows.

Noviceship
> Refers to the place where novices go through the process of formation leading to full membership; also called novitiate

NSCJ
> *Novice du Sacré-Coeur de Jésus* – Novice of the Sacred Heart of Jesus, identifying initials used until a novice makes first vows

Oakwood
> Retirement home of the Society of the Sacred Heart on the campus of Sacred Heart Schools, Atherton, California

Office, Divine Office (see Liturgy of the Hours)

Philippine (see Duchesne)

Philippine's Holy Thursday journey
> Philippine Duchesne's mystical experience, joining herself to the saving work of Christ, on the night of Holy Thursday, 1806

Postulant

Once the name for someone in her first phase of formation, asking to "come and see," from the Latin *postulare*, "to ask;" this phase of formation is now called "candidacy."

Probation

Sometimes likened to a second noviceship, "probation" is a word used in the Society to refer to a period of approximately five months spent in prayer and study with other RSCJs from around the world prior to final profession.

Probation <u>name</u>: usually a phrase from Scripture that captures the unique character of the group together in probation

Probation <u>*devise*</u>: a motto that captures a particular way of living the vows into the future given to the probation group just before their final profession

Profession

Refers to the final, public "profession" of the vows of obedience, poverty and chastity

Province

An autonomous unit of government, bound together with other provinces to form the Society of the Sacred Heart

Provincial Assembly

A consultative assembly of the members of the province convoked at least once every three years

Retreat, annual

Typically, a period of eight days of prayer; an annual opportunity to deepen one's inner life and nourish one's relationship with Christ.

Thirty Day Retreat, sometimes called "the long retreat," takes place before final profession. It follows the format of the *Spiritual Exercises of Saint Ignatius.*

RSCJ

Religieuses du Sacré-Coeur de Jésus – Religious of the Sacred Heart of Jesus.

Sainte Marie d'en Haut

The Visitation Monastery in Grenoble which Philippine entered; it was suppressed in the French Revolution; later the Society of the Sacred Heart opened a school there (1804).

Sodality
The Sodality of Our Lady, known as the Children of Mary within the Society of the Sacred Heart; an association dedicated to the honor and love of Mary and service to others.

Sophie (see Barat)

Stuart, Janet Erskine, RSCJ (1857-1914)
Sixth Superior General of the Society of the Sacred Heart, known for her commitment to spiritual growth and to educational excellence; influence well beyond the Society through her publications, especially *The Education of Catholic Girls*

Suscipe
This Latin word for "receive" is the shorthand reference for a prayer of Saint Ignatius which begins, "Take, Lord, and receive all my liberty, my memory, my understanding and my entire will, all I have and call my own."

Teresian House
A center for the elderly in Albany, New York, administered by Carmelite Sisters of the Aged and Infirm, where RSCJs have been welcomed for assisted living and skilled care

Trinità dei Monti
Once a Sacred Heart convent and school at the top of the Spanish Steps in Rome, the *Trinità* remains the home of *Mater Admirabilis*, a beloved fresco of the young Mary painted by Sister Pauline Perdrau in 1844.

Constitutions of the Society of the Sacred Heart, 1982

Prayer

17. "The spirit of the Society
is essentially based upon prayer and the interior life
since we cannot glorify the adorable
Heart of Jesus worthily
except inasmuch as we apply ourselves
to study His interior dispositions
in order to unite and conform ourselves to them."
(Abridged Plan 5)

18. Jesus calls us
to a personal encounter with Him.
He wants to make known to us
the feelings and the preferences of His Heart.

19. In the Gospel
through His words, His attitudes,
His relationships with people,
His way of relating to all created things,
we discover His Heart
wholly given to the Father and to all people.

20. In prayer we come to Him
with everything that touches our life,
with the sufferings and hopes of humanity.
We learn to remain in silence
and poverty of heart before Him
In the free gift of ourselves
we learn to adore and to abide in His love.

21. The Spirit dwelling within us
gradually transforms us, enabling us
through His power to remove whatever
hinders His action.
The Spirit unites and conforms us to Jesus
and makes us sensitive to His presence
within ourselves, in others and in all that happens.
Thus we learn to contemplate reality

and to experience it with His Heart,
to commit ourselves to the service of the Kingdom
and to grow in love:
"Have this mind among yourselves
which was in Christ Jesus" (Phil. 2:5).

22. This contemplative attitude permeates our whole being,
helping us to live ever more united to Christ
in our relationships, our tasks and our ministry;
it becomes a powerful force
of conversion and transformation for mission.
In welcoming God's word
Mary gave Christ to the world.
In receiving the life of Jesus
we give ourselves with Him so that all may have life.

23. Prayer, the contemplative outlook on the world,
union with Christ in daily living
make us grow in the interior life,
so that in all circumstances we seek
to glorify the Heart of Jesus.

24. The Society's call to contemplation,
a compelling love written in our hearts by the Spirit,
makes us seek and cherish
prolonged times of prayer.
Our relationship with Christ is nourished
by the study of Scripture, by reading,
reflection and daily examen,
all of which are necessary for the deepening
of our inner life;
this relationship is further strengthened
by periodic renewal and an annual retreat.

25. Within this common vocation,
each one receives her own unique call.
We respond to it personally
in and through our diverse cultures.
The demands of mission and our spiritual background
necessarily influence rhythms and forms of prayer.

Desiring to keep God at the centre of our lives
we are drawn to give one hour each day to prayer,
without this time being considered in any sense a limit.
Each religious finds her own rhythm of prayer
and will decide how best she is to be faithful
to what Christ asks of her and of the Society.
She will discern the method and style of her prayer-life
with a person of her own choice,
with the agreement of the provincial or someone
delegated by her.
The Society offers it members the means necessary
for their life of prayer, according to their needs:
among others

> – spiritual direction
> – reflection with a religious of the Congregation
> – help from the community
> – the assurance of the necessary time and space for prayer.

We are invited to say the rosary
and to adopt the forms of Marian devotion
proper to the country in which we live.

26. The community takes to heart the need
to create a climate
which favours experience of God,
sharing among ourselves and with others.
Each day our life together is strengthened
by community prayer.
We share the Word of God,
say the Morning and Evening Prayer of the Church
unless we have been dispensed
from this by competent authority,
and adopt forms of prayer which help us
to grow in faith, hope and love.
The Feast of the Sacred Heart is for us
a time to renew and deepen our common spirituality.
On that day, in a spirit of thanksgiving,
we renew our vows in union with the whole Society.

27. Knowing our weakness
and our involvement in the sin of the world,

we participate often in the sacrament of reconciliation.
We joyfully welcome God's mercy
which renews our hearts
and moves us to restore communion.
We prepare ourselves for this sacrament
by the daily examen. (Canon 664)

28. Whether we pray alone or with others,
our prayer is that of the People of God.
In the local church
we celebrate the mysteries of the life of Christ,
the feast of Mary and of the saints,
aware that we are members of one Body, the Church,
which worships God in prayer and song.

29. The Eucharist is the culmination of this ecclesial prayer.
As far as we can, we participate in it actively every day.
By receiving the body of Christ,
we unite ourselves to His prayer of thanksgiving
and to His offering of Himself to the Father
for the life of the world.
Gradually, the Eucharist makes us become more truly
Body of Christ, broken to give birth to a new humanity.

Contributors

Bridget Bearss, RSCJ
A native of Omaha, Nebraska, Sister Bearss followed her aunts, Eileen and Rosemary, in joining the Society. She has taught at Duchesne Academy, Houston and the Academy of the Sacred Heart, Grand Coteau, and, since 2000, she has served as head of school at the Academy of the Sacred Heart, Bloomfield Hills, Michigan.

Beatrice Brennan, RSCJ
Although Sister Brennan spent many years teaching or administering Sacred Heart schools and Manhattanville College, a "lifelong desire to serve poor people" took her to Egypt where she spent thirteen of the happiest years of her life. "Now," she says, "each day opens on a new vista of the unlimited depth of God's deep wonder."

Muriel Cameron, RSCJ
Professed in Japan in 1974, Sister Cameron served thirty-two years in Network schools, ten years as campus minister and faculty member at Creighton University, in ministry with Mexican migrant workers and in spiritual direction and retreat work. Her graduate degrees in theology are from the University of San Francisco and Creighton University.

Maureen J. Chicoine, RSCJ
Sister Chicoine transferred to the Society after twenty years in a congregation specializing in parish ministry. For eighteen years, she served as parish leader in place of a resident priest pastor in San Bernardino, California. She is now serving at Duchesne House for Volunteers in New Orleans.

Theresa Mei-fen Chu, RSCJ
Sister Chu served for fifteen years in Korea as Head of Sacred Heart institutions, followed by ten years working in a Canadian program building bridges with churches in China. After retirement, she spent fourteen happy years teaching in Catholic institutions of formation for priests and women religious in China.

Maria Cimperman, RSCJ

Sister Cimperman serves as associate professor of Theological Ethics and director of the Center for the Study of Consecrated Life at Catholic Theological Union in Chicago. Between pondering, writing and presenting, she enjoys hiking, reading, movies, time in outrageous beauty and enjoying her wonder-full niece and nephew, Maeve and Samuel.

Lillian Conaghan, RSCJ

After years of teaching in Sacred Heart schools and serving as assistant to the Superior, Sister Conaghan was invited to offer welcome and hospitality at the provincial office, a ministry she truly loved. She continues this ministry of hospitality at the Society's retirement home in California, where she also enjoys a ministry of prayer.

Margaret Ann (Margie) Conroy, RSCJ

Originally from Newfoundland, Sister Conroy has served in Africa for more than forty years. Formerly the provincial of the Uganda – Kenya Province, she also served in prison ministry and founded a Sacred Heart school for poor people in Nairobi.

Trudy Considine, RSCJ

After serving in Sacred Heart and parochial schools for twenty years, Sister Considine spent seventeen years offering direct services to the immigrant community, including co-founding SOFIA Immigration Services. More recently she has offered teaching and sacramental preparation at St. Martin de Porres, and a variety of services at Oakwood.

Suzanne Cooke, RSCJ

Sister Cooke now serves as the head of the Conference of Sacred Heart Education after serving as head of school at Carrollton in Miami, Florida for seventeen years and at Forest Ridge in Bellevue, Washington for eight years. A native New Yorker, she enjoys reading historic fiction and travel logs.

Dolores Copeland, RSCJ

Since entering the Society, Sister Copeland has taught middle school students in Washington, Philadelphia, Boston, Houston, Miami and, today, in Menlo, California. Her goal: enabling students to live a life of rich meaning and self-knowledge, with a faithful relationship with the living God.

Martha Curry, RSCJ

Sister Curry was an educator in the Network of Sacred Heart Schools and then at Duchesne and Barat colleges. She published a history of Barat College in 2012. She has also served as director of the retirement community in Albany. Now she helps RSCJ students from overseas with their reading and writing assignments.

Kathleen Dolan, RSCJ

Sister Dolan has served in several Sacred Heart Schools around the province in a variety of capacities: administrator, classroom teacher and as campus minister. She is presently working in formation to mission at Sacred Heart Schools in Atherton, California.

Jan Dunn, RSCJ

Sister Dunn has served in various roles in the Network of Sacred Heart Schools: English teacher, dean of students and headmistress at Duchesne in Omaha and Duchesne in Houston. She has twice served as interim director of the Network. She is committed to the service of education as a means of creating community.

Mary Ann (Sis) Flynn, RSCJ

Sister Flynn taught and counseled in Sacred Heart schools in the United States, Japan and Indonesia, practiced as a therapist and ended her active ministry at the Society's Spiritual Ministry Center. In retirement she helps where possible, cherishing time to reflect on a lifetime and listen to the birds sing!

Mary Frohlich, RSCJ

Sister Frohlich has taught Spirituality at Catholic Theological Union in Chicago for twenty-three years. Her publications include essays on spirituality as a discipline, Carmelite spiritual writers, and topics in ecospirituality. She is gardener of her community's large and rather wild yard, and loves to lead hiking retreats in the summer.

Joan Gannon, RSCJ

After serving in Sacred Heart Schools in Boston, Princeton and Portsmouth, Sister Gannon spent eighteen years in ministry to migrant farmworkers and refugees in Indiantown, Florida and to people with AIDS in Manhattan, followed by six years on the provincial team. Her present ministry is with her elder sisters in Albany.

Nancy Ghio, RSCJ

Sister Ghio entered the Society in the former Southern Province and moved from one school to another: City House, St Charles, Villa Duchesne and the Rosary, teaching in the primary grades before moving to the middle school as *surveillante*. She has recently completed her fiftieth year as a Sacred Heart educator.

Frances M. Gimber, RSCJ

After many years working in Sacred Heart schools, Sister Gimber was called to the secretariat of the motherhouse in Rome. She has been provincial archivist. She now shares her knowledge of the Society's history and traditions, gives talks, translates and edits Society materials.

Carol Haggarty, RSCJ

Much of Sister Haggarty's life has been spent in teaching and administration, including nine years as head of the Academy of the Sacred Heart in Grand Coteau, ten years as assistant director of the Network of Sacred Heart Schools and, currently, assistant to the provincial. She is also an avid photographer.

Linda Hayward, RSCJ

After studies at the Jesuit School of Theology in Berkeley, Sister Hayward engaged in parish ministry, especially RCIA, in both the San Francisco and San Diego dioceses. She now works with the Ignatian Volunteer Corps and the Interfaith Committee for Worker Justice, does spiritual direction, grows African violets, and writes.

Ellen Hoffman, RSCJ

Sister Hoffman had a gift for working with young children, first at Sheridan Road, Chicago and then at the Convent of the Sacred Heart and Stuart Hall in San Francisco, preparing hundreds of children for First Communion. In old age she continued sharing her love and grateful spirit at Oakwood, dying at 98 on January 19, 2015.

Mary Hotz, RSCJ

After teaching in the Network of Sacred Heart Schools and completing graduate work at the University of Chicago, Sister Hotz, in 1996, joined the English Department at the University of San Diego, where she teaches courses in Victorian studies and Native-American literatures.

Kathleen Hughes, RSCJ

After serving in Sacred Heart Schools in Washington and Boston, Sister Hughes spent nineteen years teaching liturgy, sacraments and preaching at the Catholic Theological Union at Chicago followed by six years in provincial leadership. She now spends her time writing and speaking, and perfecting her recipe for Christmas candy.

Nancy C. Kehoe, RSCJ

For twenty-three years Sister Kehoe had a private psychotherapy practice. In 1981, she began groups on spirituality in psychiatric day treatment programs, a pioneer endeavor at the time. Her book, *Wrestling with Our Inner Angels: Faith, Mental Illness and the Journey to Wholeness*, captures her work.

Kimberly M. King, RSCJ

To date, Sister King has spent twelve years in the Network of Sacred Heart Schools as a librarian and a classroom teacher. She has published poetry, maintains a blog, and has taught many kids how to juggle. Fluent in Spanish, Sister King has also translated at international meetings.

Joan Kirby, RSCJ

Sister Kirby was headmistress at Sacred Heart schools in Princeton and New York before joining the Temple of Understanding to foster interfaith dialogue. She designed an immersion program in seven religious traditions, represented the Temple at the United Nations and was a founding member of the Interfaith Consortium for Ecological Civilization.

Mary (Be) Mardel, RSCJ

Sister Mardel has spent most of her religious life at Schools of the Sacred Heart, San Francisco, as teacher, superior and director of schools. Superior at El Cajon in the 1960s and provincial of the western province in the 1970s, she moved to Oakwood in 2004 and has found that the Lord has "saved the best wine to the last."

Kathleen McGrath, RSCJ

Sister McGrath is a trained spiritual director and has experience in companioning others in the Spiritual Exercises of St. Ignatius in English and Spanish. She holds master's degrees in business and theology and worked for fifteen years with men and women who were homeless in New York City, Chicago, Boston and St. Louis.

Jane McKinlay, RSCJ

A native San Franciscan, Sister McKinlay has been at Sophie Barat House in New Orleans since 1994, facilitating spiritual growth groups and meeting with individuals wanting congruence between their spirituality and day-to-day life. She volunteers with the Fourth World Movement (partnering with the poorest to eliminate poverty). Saints football is her favorite diversion.

Margaret Mary (Marg) Miller, RSCJ

Sister Miller has served in teaching, provincial governance, group facilitation, music and retreat ministry in the United States, Canada and the Province of Uganda/Kenya. Currently, she lives and ministers in Atherton, California.

Shirley Miller, RSCJ

Sister Miller served as teacher and administrator in the Network of Sacred Heart Schools from 1968-2003 at Woodlands, Duchesne, Omaha and the Academy of the Sacred Heart, New Orleans (the Rosary). She has served as Director of Mission Advancement for the Society since 2004.

Marcia O'Dea, RSCJ

Sister O'Dea has for the past forty years taught high school English at Forest Ridge School of the Sacred Heart. While her primary love is the teaching of British Literature, she appreciates leading students to "write well." She enjoys singing in the adult choir of the school - and reading mysteries!

Uchenna Oluoha, NSCJ

Sister Oluoha, a native of Nigeria and an American citizen, worked as a registered nurse in a cardiac care unit of Kaiser Permanente Hospital in Northern California before joining the Society of the Sacred Heart in 2013. She is currently in initial formation.

Virginia (Gin) O'Meara, RSCJ

Sister O'Meara was an educator and administrator in Sacred Heart schools and professor at Maryville College, St. Louis. The 1970s saw her focus shift to the creativity of silk screening, painting, pottery, papermaking, photography, weaving and poetry, all informed by her study of Carl Jung. She died in 2005.

Carolyn (Lyn) Osiek, RSCJ

Sister Osiek spent thirty-two years teaching graduate biblical studies. She is now provincial archivist and continues to do some writing and teaching in biblical studies as she prepares the writings of Saint Philippine for publication.

Clare Pratt, RSCJ

Sister Pratt, a native of Washington, DC, worked in Sacred Heart, public and parochial schools on the East Coast and in Houston, Texas. She served in Society administration in the United States and Rome, including eight years as Superior General. She is currently community life director of the Society's retirement community in Atherton, California.

Rose Marie Quilter, RSCJ

Teaching, pastoral ministry, and practicing therapeutic massage prepared Sister Quilter for her current ministry, Dreams Without Borders, at ARISE in the Rio Grande Valley of Texas. There, she conducts classes in alternative health, teaches basic English to adult immigrants and is part of a staff which serves 2,500 immigrant families.

Barbara Quinn, RSCJ

Sister Quinn is currently the associate director for spiritual formation at the Boston College School of Theology and Ministry after serving at the University of San Diego for ten years. Her ministries have included formation work, spiritual direction and retreats, teaching, and designing and administering ministry development programs for laity.

Mary Patricia Rives, RSCJ

Sister Rives was born in Mexico, grew up in San Antonio, and attended the Rosary and the College of the Sacred Heart, Grand Coteau, Louisiana. She has served in Sacred Heart schools in Missouri, Ohio, Louisiana and Texas, and presently ministers as school nurse at Villa Duchesne and Oak Hill School in St. Louis.

Diane Roche, RSCJ

Sister Roche has spent nearly forty years living and working in poor neighborhoods from Seattle to Haiti; affordable housing, community development, and the environment preoccupy her. Currently director of the Office of Justice, Peace and Integrity of Creation at the Stuart Center, she is also a member of the Vocation Outreach Team.

Pierina (Rina) Ronconi, RSCJ

Born in Italy in 1913, Rina recognized her vocation at an early age. After surviving World War II in Rome, she came to the United States, where she sewed habits and served in the vestries and cafeterias at Sacred Heart schools in El Cajon, Menlo Park and San Francisco, California.

Helen Rosenthal, RSCJ

From Rome to Chile, Sister Rosenthal spent twenty years as a missionary. With a doctorate in historical theology she began the Spirituality Center at St. Thomas University in Florida; she chaired the history, philosophy and religious studies department and created the online International Spirituality Program. Recently retired, she continues her daily blog.

Marianne T. Ruggeri, RSCJ

Sister Ruggeri is a clinical psychologist with a private practice on Cape Cod. Before beginning her doctoral studies, she served for twenty-eight years in several Sacred Heart schools.

Oonah Ryan, RSCJ

Sister Ryan worked with students for sixteen years in schools as diverse as the Convent of the Sacred Heart, Greenwich and Harlem Prep School. She served as retreat director and counselor and now works as an artist and co-director of a neighborhood artisan organization that benefits families at risk.

Mary Schumacher, RSCJ

Sister Schumacher spent twenty years in parish ministry and another twenty years in counseling. Her last employment was at the Betty Ford Center. She is currently facilitating retreats and spiritual direction, and enjoys photography as a member of the Camera Club.

Patricia Shaffer, RSCJ

After teaching at Sacred Heart Schools, Atherton, 1952-57, and obtaining her MS at Stanford University and her PhD in chemistry from UC-San Diego, Sister Shaffer served on the faculty at the University of San Diego, 1959-1999, and then helped out on the USD campus while she carried out research at San Diego State.

Regina Shin, RSCJ

A native of Korea, Sister Shin came to the United States in 1988 and entered the Society ten years later. An artist who has also studied computer graphics and spiritual direction, her exceptional organizational skills have been utilized, most recently, as a member of the provincial staff.

Sheila Smith, RSCJ

Sheila Smith comes from a long line of spiritual, creative, and activist women. She also inherited from her family a deep love for nature and intercultural exchange between peoples. Sister Smith is a lifelong learner and community scholar, currently engaged in initiatives to support the resurgence of Indigenous learning in Canada.

Anne Sturges, RSCJ

Having taught in Sacred Heart schools in Albany and Connecticut, and serving as campus minister at Manhattanville College, Sister Sturges worked sixteen years as pastoral associate in Bronx parishes. For the past twenty years, she has been a hospice chaplain in New Orleans, where she now coordinates Sacred Heart Associates.

Mary Jane Sullivan, RSCJ

After teaching for twenty years in Sacred Heart Schools, Sister Sullivan moved into parish ministry in Boston and then San Francisco, focusing on adult faith formation and liturgy. "Retirement" included service with Associates, alumnae and others. Presently she lives in Albany, happily assisting with care of our elder sisters.

Stephany Veluz, RSCJ

Sister Veluz lives in San Diego, California and has been a member of the Spiritual Ministry Center Team since 2011, doing retreat work and spiritual direction. She is also a student of the Zen Center in San Diego, and she enjoys the beauty of nature, walking and reading.

Deanna Rose von Bargen, RSCJ

Mostly a God-fanatic, Sister von Bargen has dabbled in Montessori education, oil painting, violin, retreat ministry, adult faith formation, liturgy, softball, croquet and bowling with young adults who also came to bible study. Currently she journeys with adult Native American Indians, conducting fun classes in sacraments and the bible. She reads a lot.

Anne Wachter, RSCJ

After nine years at Sacred Heart schools in Omaha, New York, Lake Forest and Grand Coteau, Sister Wachter studied Spanish in Mexico, completed a Master's at the University of San Francisco, and served for fifteen years as an administrator at Convent of the Sacred Heart, San Francisco. In 2012, she was named headmistress of the Sacred Heart School in Halifax.

Mary Pat White, RSCJ

After serving in Network Schools in St. Charles, St. Louis and Houston, Sister White served in several Newman Centers at universities in California. She was director of the Service and Immersion Program at Duchesne House for Volunteers in New Orleans. Presently, she serves as vocation director for the United States – Canada Province.

Credits

28417743R00094

Made in the USA
Middletown, DE
14 January 2016